BUS TO

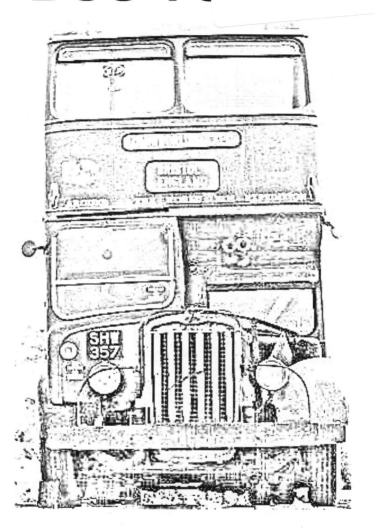

John Winter

ISBN: 9798372828919

I compiled a diary as I travelled with my companions through North and South America and that forms the basis of this book. I added more thoughts over the years and the bus crew made hugely useful contributions, which I was delighted to include and for which I am very grateful.

For many of us as we get older memories and impressions become like snowflakes that either settle or drift away and could be lost for ever.

You have to make a grab for them as they pass and compose them into something solid and lasting.

It is a battle that sometimes we lose. That's why a proportion of any profits from Bus To Bust will go to research into dementia and the dreadful Alzheimer's disease.

My thanks to graphic designer Marc Bessant for his excellent cover image and to editor and publisher Peter Gibbs for the enthusiasm that revived this book.

CONTENTS

Foreword & The Planned Route...................................6

The Bus...7

The Crew..8

Chapter One...10

Chapter Two...15

Chapter Three...27

Chapter Four..37

Chapter Five..44

Chapter Six...56

Chapter Seven...75

Chapter Eight...80

Chapter Nine..94

Chapter Ten..102

Chapter 11...119

Chapter 12...139

Chapter 13...148

Chapter 14...158

Chapter 15...172

Chapter 16...183

Chapter 17...192

Chapter 18..201

Chapter 19..205

Chapter 20..217

Chapter 21..224

Chapter 22..235

Chapter 23..244

The Actual Route..256

Chapter 24..258

Media Coverage...272

Images: Dave McLaughlin and Mike Conway

Foreword

In 1970, Avonmouth docks policeman Roger Poole decided to put together a group to circumnavigate the globe in a Bristol double-decker bus, financing the journey by selling British goods as they travelled from continent to continent.

That was the plan.

This is their remarkable story, told here in amazing detail for the first time.

The Planned Route

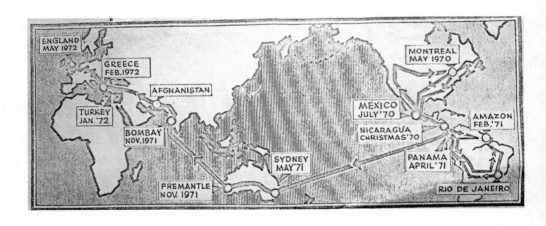

The Bus - SHW 357

Double-decker delivered in January, 1955, to Bristol Tramways & Carriage Company, later Bristol Omnibus Company Ltd.

Aluminium body by Eastern Coach Works of Lowestoft - length: 27 feet; height: 14 feet, 6 inches; width: 8 feet.

Seating: 32 upstairs, 28 downstairs. Rear platform with enclosed manually-operated two-piece doors and saloon heaters.

Powered by Gardner 6LW diesel engine, 6 cylinders in line, capacity 8.4 litres, output between 102 and 112 bhp, with a 5-speed manual gearbox and no power steering.

After serving bus routes throughout Bristol, SHW 357 moved to Bath in December, 1961, but was withdrawn from service in 1969.

In 14 years of passenger-carrying the double-decker travelled an estimated 770,000 miles.

Statistics supplied by Dr Mike Walker, Bristol Omnibus Vehicle Collection

The Crew

 Roger Poole, aged 23, Avonmouth Docks police constable

 Bernice Poole, aged 23, secretary at the South West Regional Hospital Board in Bristol

 Mike Conway, aged 29, caterer at a Bristol hospital

 David McLaughlin, aged 27, ex-Royal Artillery

 Bob Cooke, aged 23, lift engineer

 Jan Clarke, aged 19, working in the advertising section of the Bristol Evening Post

John Winter, aged 26, journalist at the Bristol Evening Post

 Sally Rich, aged 23, State Registered Nurse

 Peter Conway, aged 24, delivery driver

 Don Coles, aged 39, painter and decorator

 Joan Coles, aged 37, GPO telephonist

CHAPTER ONE

GRADUALLY, out of the shimmering heat, a vehicle appeared; big, red, an intrusion into the barren landscape. As it approached, the curious spectator could see a bus, a double-decker, bigger and noisier than the single-deckers they sometimes saw in that part of the world.

It threw up a cloud of dirt and dust as it passed.

It shouldn't have been there, thousands of miles from England.

Then, it was gone.

It made little lasting impact in the small towns and remote places across North America, and in Mexico, Colombia, and Peru, apart from knocking down the occasional overhead power line or grazing the underside of a low bridge.

But it stayed on in the memory of those who saw it and wondered: Where did it come from? Why? Who was on it?

This is the story of that big, red double-decker.

This is not a children's story, and if you try reading it to them they will soon lose interest, hopefully before Chapter Five when things get a bit frisky.

I did try (and fail) to write a children's story in an idle moment on the road (somewhere between Houston and Mexico City), try (and fail), with rough (very rough) cartoons, but my literary deliberations were interrupted by the shouts of a cop as that big red double-decker bus collided with a bunch of telephone wires that were now hanging waist-high across the middle of a busy street.

This bus, our bus, had long ago left Bristol, England, where it had already covered 770,000 miles of roads dutifully carrying local people.

It was now part-way through a journey that took it past Cape Canaveral with its towering Moon rocket launch pads, through Mexican wastelands where kids washed in streams, over ice fields in Canada and treacherous mountain passes in South America.

We were 11 men and women, most in our twenties, who in 1970/71 shared the experience of attempting to travel around the world on this bouncing, rattling beast.

We each saw the experience differently, and often hated one another. Ray Davies, who knew a bit about touring with the same group of people for months on end (The Kinks were legendary for fighting each other on stage), described it thus: "You needed one another, but you didn't always like each other."

That sums it up nicely.

We all have different tales to tell. I have to concentrate on how I saw it.

We were in the USA on our bus in 1970 and 1971. Nixon was President, the Vietnam War protests were at their height, Charles Manson was on trial for the Sharon Tate killings and decimalisation was being introduced back home in the UK.

We drove thousands of miles to Mexico for the World Cup soccer finals, arriving after England had been knocked out, and thousands more to deepest Peru en route to disaster. Paddington Bear had already made many friends in Britain, but had yet to meet the Queen.

Our relatives and friends were out of touch for births, serious illnesses, financial crises and all the other stresses and strains and joys of everyday life. No email. There was no Internet to link the different countries and cultures. Mobile phones and Sat Navs were not even a glint in an entrepreneurial eye.

To phone home was expensive and public phones were not easy to find. I was away two years in North America and Mexico and managed to phone home three times, and one resulted in a wrong number.

Our world was inside that double-decker bus.

It was a very small world.

Back then double-deckers rattled even more than they do today, and belched fumes as though it were compulsory. Ever imagined what it would be like to eat, sleep go to the loo and shave on one (no, not at the same time). And we had a honeymoon couple on board!

A double-decker bus is a heavy, low base, awkward vehicle to move around. If you are not on an even road surface, it gets difficult.

On uneven or wet ground it is less manoeuvrable than a whale in quicksand. We planned to take it across deserts and through ice fields, up mountains and into deep river valleys.

Ever heard the expression 'You could get a double-decker bus through there'? Well, events proved that we could (until that fateful last day!). Once, we even managed to bump-start it!

Our home was a goldfish bowl, people looking in, 11 of us staring out.

And it was a small world because we had one driving force that excluded everything else: to make enough money, and to overcome all the physical obstacles and personal conflicts that might stop us carrying on around the world.

Our first stop was the 1970 World Cup. England soccer fans had good reason to be confident. We were, after all, the World Cup holders!

Eleven of us started the trip, but by the time the bus reached Colombia five had left.

Now, three have died, one is in Australia, one lives in the Orkney islands, two have completely lost touch, and the rest are back in England.

Older, greyer, some a bit heavier, probably not changed much in attitude since we returned from our adventure.

We were two years older when we returned, but it had been fun and an adventure.

The aim had been to make enough money from manual work - mostly in the fruit fields - and whatever jobs we could find to pay for our day-to-day travel expenses.

We had some hope at the outset that advertisers would contribute a decent proportion of the costs by paying for space on the side of the bus, but that hardly materialised

Sometimes the press would describe us as students, but we were not. Nor were we hippies. We all had regular professions back home, a cop, a chef, a nurse and so on. We got together to share an experience.

We drifted from place to place, staying where we made money, or sometimes friends. Bouncing along on roads so bad that is it difficult to stand upright, and to get from the top deck it was best to squirm down the stairs on your backside.

Even though a lot of the time we were knackered from climbing trees to pick fruit, and a lot of the rest we were bored sick trying to pass the time playing Monopoly as the bus bumped its way along highways, freeways and dirt tracks, it was fun.

It was fun when the skies rained on us for the first time in two months (being British, we missed the rain) and we pulled over and stood on a dusty Oregon highway soaking it in; and, yes, fun emptying the chemical toilet, a little procession, someone in front holding a large shovel with which to dig the hole, followed by two carrying the aforementioned gleaming white vestibule, and a fourth armed with a large stick with which to beat "any that were still kicking!"

The bus went through deserts and icefields and up mountains – setting an altitude record of 12,000 feet for such a vehicle - and on and on across continents at a steady 35mph, or more with a following wind. The only thing that threatened to halt it was lack of money for diesel.

A big red bus. The first Big Brother. Who would leave next?

A very small world.

This is how it happened.

CHAPTER TWO

Throw the bus into reverse, with a clang and a shudder. It didn't do reverse very willingly.

It's April 1970: In the back garden of a semi in Filton, Bristol, stood a partly red, partly green double-decker bus, surrounded by planks and engine bits and a large glass-fibre water tank. Someone was working on the platform, another painting the roof red, and hammering could be heard from the inside.

"What's all the noise?" someone asked a neighbour.

"They are off to Mexico in that bus, to see the World Cup..."

Actually, we weren't just off to Mexico City to watch England defend the crown won in 1966. We were planning a trip around the world, and Mexico would be the first stop.

Eleven youngish people, two couples and seven singles, determined that our 1955 bus would overcome any terrain and any climate so that we could support our country's soccer team - the Champions.

Well, that was the boys' aim, anyway. The girls were not that bothered with the soccer. They wanted to see the world.

We knew it would be a tough task to get to Mexico City on time, via Montreal, New York State, Texas and the unpredictable Mexican roads. We didn't mind being a bit late.

"Being world champions we were convinced that we didn't need to be there for the early rounds as we were bound to get through," explained Roger Poole, the leader of the group.

"Only Bristol Rovers supporters like me and Bob (Cooke) could be that stupidly optimistic."

And we hoped to make enough money from selling British goods or working in the fruit fields to keep us on the road.

We needed luck, we needed to work together as a unit, and most of all we needed the bus - which from the front with its big upper windows and wide radiator might look like a grinning British bulldog - to overcome road and climate conditions that it had never experienced in hundreds of thousands of miles of commercial service at home.

Looking back, we displayed breath-taking naivety in assuming that we would be able to complete the trip and not be left stranded somewhere with no money and no hope of getting home, but when you are young you are convinced you are invincible, and that whatever happened we would muddle through.

We were mostly complete strangers.

It was Roger's idea. Blame him. Or maybe Bernice, his fiancée.

Roger Poole, 23, a policeman, and Bernice Peglar, 23, who decided they wanted to fulfil an ambition to travel, and advertised in the Bristol Evening Post for people to join them on a trip around the world - on a bus. They didn't mention it would be their honeymoon!

Before we start, let's make it clear that Roger was the leader and without him the trip would never have become a reality, nor would we have covered so much ground over the next two years.

It could, and should be said, that Roger – who was to become one of the country's leading trade unionists and top political negotiators – fine-tuned the leadership skills that would later have such an impact on industrial relations in dealing with the different and conflicting personalities on the bus, and the problems we encountered.

When he died at the age of 69 in July 2015, the Guardian described him as having become "the acceptable face of trade unionism at the end of the bitterly-divided 1980s."

It was a remarkable achievement, one of many Roger attained. He was a leader of men and would have made a great politician. I met him many times after we all returned to England, and was honoured to be his friend.

However, back to the early stages of organising a double-decker bus trip around the world….

"I suppose that Bern and I, who met on Christmas night 1963, were not ready to settle down to 9 to 5 jobs, get married and have a family," Roger told me later.

"We both had itchy feet and in our different ways were searching for something unusual to do. The idea of the bus absolutely did NOT come from the film, Summer Holiday (Cliff Richards was the wholesome leader of a wholesome crew) although many people assume it did.

"We eventually decided that travelling was what we wanted to do and knew that if we were going to do it and see parts of the world that travellers only rarely see we would have to do it over an extended period of time and do it cheaply. We had no money."

Bernice added: "My idea had been a single decker stripped out and installed with ex-army bunk beds purchased from Exchange and Mart (remember them). Oh no, says Roger, far too boring, has to be a double-decker to make more impact because he already had this idea of using Harold Wilson's 'We're backing Britain' mantra to make money from the journey by promoting British goods.

"We approached Bristol Commercial Vehicles and were quoted £250 for a double-decker bus in good condition. Roger decided on a high-decker, which was some inches higher than the low-decker - this bus, of course, ultimately made our lives and journey much more difficult."

The low-decker at 13 feet, 6 inches was in fact a full foot shorter –
a comfortable two inches less than the maximum height allowed in
North America at the time.

And consequently our newly-acquired high-decker was to leave a
trail of damaged overhead bridges, power cables and telephone
lines wherever it went!

Next, Roger and Bernice wanted a bus crew. At the first attempt to
advertise, eight people came forward, but seven promptly dropped
out, leaving just Roger, Bernice and Mike Conway, aged 29.

He was divorced with two children and had in 1960 enjoyed a
summer in Majorca running an English-style tea rooms with his
twin brother, John, having travelled there on Vespa scooters, via
Belgium Luxembourg France Andorra and Spain.

They returned in late autumn, broke as always. Now working as
Catering Officer in a large Bristol hospital, Mike had a career "but
nothing to strive for." He said he sought adventure; we suspected
he was also looking for a new wife.

Roger and Bernice advertised again; they wanted people with
specific skills, not just a yen to travel. They knew that in South
American jungles and disease-ridden villages they would need to
be self-sufficient in many ways.

Health was a priority so they needed a nurse. Mechanics were
also urgently needed - Roger had been a mechanic, but he knew
that in the trying conditions they would encounter they would need
more than one pair of hands to lug out the gearbox of an English
bus.

Sally Rich, 23, a State Registered Nurse, and Bob Cooke, 23, a lift
mechanic, were selected to fill these roles.

Sally proved to be inexhaustible. She was always early to rise (even if she had been out socialising half the night), and had cleaned the downstairs living area before the rest of us joined her.

She was full of good humour. Sal was made of stern stuff – she was brought up on a hill farm in the middle of Dartmoor and so had a very isolated upbringing – no electricity for many years and water was from a spring on the moors.

She had always wanted to travel, but not until she finished training as a nurse. To raise the money she felt she needed for the trip, Sal worked six nights a week, got rid of her flat and slept on a friend's floor.

Bob also had an appealing easy-going manner, but could be very determined, even obstinate, which was useful particularly if he was struggling to sort out a similarly inflexible mechanical problem, under the bus. He was often covered in oil, usually grinning.

Bob had developed a taste for travel. After completing five years in lift engineering, he emigrated to South Africa, but after less than a year, unable to accept apartheid, he returned to the UK. His parents saw the ad and he applied to join the group. "They took me in to their flock. I was right, they were desperate," he joked.

Dave McLaughlin, 27, ex Royal Artillery, joined to organise navigation and be one of the bus drivers. He had just completed a 10-year hitch with the Royal Artillery. He had served in Germany (three times), the Outer Hebrides and Gibraltar before taking his option to leave.

He recalls: "I returned to Bristol and wandered into the Employment Exchange to see the military employment advisor. We had a chat and he gave me a job in their office to start on the following Monday. It was casual but gave me something to do. Soon after I saw an advert about a bus going on a world tour. I applied and that is now history."

Another driver would be Don Coles, an interior decorator, formerly in the Army, who, with his wife, Joan, had started a similar tour that had fallen through.

They said they were in their early 30s, but I think they were actually older than that – 42 years later Don said he was 80!

They were to prove a great asset – Don big and dependable, intimidating if you needed it, and Joan always motherly and willing to do the dirty jobs.

Jan Clarke, aged 19, who had recently lost her Dad after her Mum died some time before, was an advertising saleswoman for the Bristol Evening Post and was picked to handle promotions from which the group hoped to make some money.

Mike's brother, Peter, aged 24, was a long-distance lorry driver, who was picked because of his driving experience and mechanical knowledge.

Bernice, a secretary, took over the finances and administrative work. Red-haired, with a fiery personality, she was to prove one of the backbones of the trip, adopting a no-nonsense approach that complemented her fiance, Roger's more subtle approach to making the project work.

Roger apparently always planned to include a journalist, because it would be handy for getting the publicity they needed around the world.

That was me, who went to interview the group for a story to appear in the Bristol Evening Post and was rapidly hooked.

At this point I want to demonstrate how different life was in those days, and how out of reach North America, let alone Mexico, seemed to ordinary people, who did not have the benefit of watching news and documentaries about foreign countries on TV.

When I began to write this, The Queen had overtaken Queen Victoria as the longest reigning British monarch, after more than 63 years on the throne, yet I clearly remember the day her father, King George VI, died in 1952.

It was announced at assembly at Gatten and Lake School and Pauline Pitfield cried. She was seven like me. I remember hearing the never-ending mournful music on the radio.

We didn't have TV in those days; in fact I clearly recall my Mum saying to go next door because our neighbours had invited me to look at their television, the first in our street - I went outside, stood on a grassy bank opposite our homes, looked up at the aerial, and went back to my Mum saying: "I can't see any pictures."

We grew up with radio, not TV, but we started to learn more about countries across the sea with the start of foreign holidays, mostly to France or Spain, and that whetted our appetite for more travel. I was 26 when I embarked on the bus adventure, but basically still a small-town boy.

But let's start my story in 1960 when I was a reporter on the Isle of Wight Guardian, and you can't get a smaller newspaper than that, covering every death in Shanklin (which meant adopting as much of a hang-dog look as I could muster to get biographic details from relatives - "would you like to see him? We've laid him out nicely on the table.") It was all part of the job.

Then there was shivering on touchlines at local football matches, lusting after the show girls at Sandown Pier on the first night of the summer season, and pestering the police for details of every minor accident and burglary.

I was 16, straight from school, a lad who was directed to the deceased's nearest and dearest by the local undertaker and don't forget to put his name at the end of the story, and don't leave out any of the floral tributes. It was a busy weekly newspaper office; the editor and her two dogs (newshounds), and me.

Now what this has to do with this story isn't that clear, not even to me, but I suppose it paints a picture – small seaside resort, highlights of the year the annual visit of the Swedish students (the girls, not the spotty youths) and the opening of the pier show, impressing the chorus girls with the fluidity of your pen, or something like that.

The beautiful, blonde Swedish girls were said to be of easy virtue, but I was never able to get close enough to find out. One girl did tell me how to say 'I love you' in Swedish (Jag älskar dig) but I never used it for fear that she had been deliberately misleading me, and that I would in fact be saying: 'My trousers are on fire.'

It was a great time to be a teenager; the birth of rock and roll, transistor radios, cheap records and dance halls jumping to new dances like the Twist. I never could get my balance trying to do the twist with a pint in my hand.

We lads (all in suits, and sometimes winklepickers) used to gather in a group near the bar trying to get up courage to ask the girls to dance, or sometimes we didn't bother.

I remember one chap, Pete Dicks who used to wear a trilby all the time, even on the dance floor, a Robin Hood hat we called it, and I didn't find it odd, but it was, of course, because he was mostly bald and that was not as fashionable as it is now. I went to his house once and said to his mum: "Hello Mrs Cox."

I nearly forgot to mention another highlight of the year - the return after the summer holidays of the girls of a posh private girls' school at Bembridge, who at the stroke of midnight scrambled out of their nighties and into something looser and warmer and dropped out of their bedroom windows into the waiting arms of the even more acne-scarred Island youths, who rushed them off in their battered Minis and Morris Oxford estates to the top of Bembridge Down to pursue foul deeds.

Why these well-bred young ladies from some of the best families in England, the Middle East and the USA should want to mix with the local rough I don't know. But it often seems to happen.

I grew up in the Isle of Wight, and had the occasional trip to Portsmouth with my dad and brothers to see Pompey play at Fratton Park (we on the island were all Pompey fans in those days, no-one supported Southampton!).

I travelled over to the mainland occasionally to meet girlfriends, but never thought about moving from the island until about 1965 when I was 21 and had the chance to meet (and drink with) students from all over the country, when my brother, Bob, invited me to stay with him for the occasional weekend at Reading University – he even very generously allowed me to use his bed one night while he slept in the bath!

So, bruised but inspired by relationship with island girls, slightly bored with covering small town stories and enticed by the sophistication of Reading (!), I decided to move to the mainland, where in those days there were plenty of jobs for everyone, not the least journalists. Certainly more than in the Isle of Wight.

I moved around the South from job to job, from Bishop's Stortford to Tonbridge, Tonbridge to Chatham, Chatham to Bristol, in three years.

I drank loads of beer and went out with lots of girls. At Bishop's Stortford I lived in a bungalow – the address was Dingley Dell, Bells Hill. It wasn't far from a teacher training college and I only had to mention the address and the young women students wanted to have a look. It wasn't that quaint and the bed collapsed.

My first experience of foreign adventure was to hitch my way to a ferry port, cross the Channel, and then hitch to Amsterdam. I wore a bowler hat and had a huge Union Jack on my case. No-one would pick me up.

At immigration they said the £13 I had on me was not enough, and they only let me through because I said I had an uncle in Amsterdam (I didn't). The first night I slept on the pavement, and the last three days I lived on chips and mayonnaise. I had a great time.

Eventually, and despite appalling shorthand, I managed to get a job on the Bristol Evening Post and hold it down long enough to be there at the right moment in 1970 when the news desk needed someone to cover the story of a group of people planning a trip around the world in a double-decker bus.

I became instantly infected with their enthusiasm, and, next minute I am in the middle of a riot in Mexico City at the end of the World Cup, and then shaking Ronald Reagan's hand, and in between getting to know lots more girls across two continents and doing a lot of fruit picking to keep us in petrol and cornflakes.

I was able to file regular reports for the paper before and after departure. I never did drive the bus. It would have been no good asking me to help the mechanics; on one occasion in the 1960s I snapped off the radiator bleed taps on two firm's Minivans in one morning (I was trying to drain out the fluid to put in anti-freeze).

I haven't improved. I still say mudguard when I mean bumper bar. In fact, given my lack of handiness I wonder they didn't consider me a safety hazard.

Publicity was important because we had in mind two main ways to raise money to meet our day-to-day expenses - working as a group, particularly in the fruit fields, and promoting or advertising goods, particularly British goods, for which we would be paid huge sums!

The Board of Trade had been very helpful (Roger found Civil Servants who tried to help, not hinder as they usually did), as were the CBI, and we had contacted a number of UK companies for samples, which we would promote in exchange for being paid commission on the subsequent sales.

Roger had organised all this when he was off shift at his job as a police constable at Avonmouth Docks - previously he had been an apprentice motor mechanic, another bonus.

The International Police Association police card he carried with him across North America subsequently got us out of many scrapes in the USA, particularly when we came upon low bridges - and made us many friends in the police.

Bernice recalls: "I really don't know how Roger came to get appointments with the CBI and Board of Trade, but he was regularly tootling off in our old Ford Anglia to London to persuade them we could save the country from ruin by promoting British goods on our travels around the world - a percentage commission would help our funding.

"They were duly on board and managed to find companies to take part - Caris Jewellery in Cornwall, Perdisan chemical toilets (free toilet), Dexion Angle (free tubing to build our wonderful extending table), Ripper Robots, which were rubber teats for milking cows (sadly they didn't get us much business but did get Mike his nickname of Ripper due to him finding them)."

Thus, when we left, we had among other items, a chemical toilet the sales pitch for which was "Princess Anne's bum has sat on one of these or that's what we were told." Potential customers could have a good look at our shiny white toilet as long as no-one was sitting on it at the time.

We had horse brasses, pewter beer mugs, costume jewellery and packaging systems, as well, would you believe, as a railway signalling system, yep for real trains, that Mike thought we could sell in India.

And as a starting fund, we had each put in £200 – not much you say, but in today's money that's getting on for a whopping £4,000!

CHAPTER THREE

On January 3rd 1970 we took delivery of our 1955 Gardner Diesel 8.4-litre engine double-decker from Bristol Omnibus Company, purchased for £250. The company were very supportive from the start, including sending spares out when we encountered a mechanical crisis (which was often).

We also should mention that a lot of companies in Bristol gave us supplies to do the bus up and equip us.

It was the start of four months of extremely hard work. The interior of the bus was completely torn apart and the normal entrance and exit doors sealed up. Thereafter we gained access through the emergency door at the rear of the bus. On the platform we built a shower and installed the toilet.

All Bristol buses were green in those days, but we decided to paint it red because that was the popular image of British buses abroad, like our pillar boxes.

All the conversion work was carried out in Mike's back garden,
which caused quite a stir amongst the neighbours.

**The Conversion Crew (l-r) Jan, Pete, Vic Webb, Roger, Bernice, Bob,
Dave and, on bus, Sally and Mike**

Our ace card was Joan's brother, Vic Webb, who was a brilliant carpenter and got our lads building bunks and beds, as well as storage seats downstairs around a large extending table and fitting our small kitchen with sliding doors to turn into a washroom.

For six months he was a star and we also owe a big thank you to his family, who rarely saw him during that time. Dave's sister, Liz, spent days glued to a sewing machine, cutting, making and hanging our curtains.

Two tanks containing 70 gallons of water were placed at the rear of the top deck (Don and Joan slept on top of it, a sort of early water bed!) feeding a kitchen sink next to the platform below, where there was also a fridge and propane cooker, sealed off by sliding doors from the rest of the lower deck which was converted into a large living room with folding tables, gas lights, and seating for up to 15 people.

The seats were removable and spare parts placed beneath them - not an inch of space was wasted!

Then we had to arrange the sleeping accommodation.

One early snag was the fact that by November, 1969, Bernice realised that her mum and dad – he was Bristol City Alderman Bert Peglar - would not be happy with her travelling on the bus with Roger unless they were married.

"It may have been the 1960s, but the old folk still had not caught up with the new world" she said. "So as well as buying the bus, converting it and planning the journey, I now had the additional task of planning our wedding, which included making my own wedding dress.

"I often teased Roger that the only reason he agreed to the marriage was because he thought that sharing a double-decker bus with nine other folk for an extended honeymoon might be a good advertising ploy."

So they were married on April 24, 1970, at Bristol's Quakers Friars register office with all the rest of the crew in attendance.

Bernice recalls: 'The end of a seven-year courtship and we finally decided to marry and share our honeymoon on a double-decker bus, travelling the world, with nine others!

'Decision made,(and after picking parents up off of floor) I had three months to make my wedding dress, organise the small but wonderful) wedding at Quakers Friars, a small reception on a houseboat at Fishponds Lido and a weekend in Cornwall before embarking on the long (although sadly not long enough) momentous life as soul mates.

'Je ne regrette rien! ....Oh, and we had to get the train home from Cornwall as our borrowed car broke down - ominous?'

31

The upper deck of the bus was converted into sleeping accommodation, two rows of single, two-storey bunk beds with a corridor between, and now, with two married couples on board, two double beds were built, one as previously mentioned at the rear, and the other (it folded down) at the front for the honeymooners. Curtains provided a little privacy (not much!).

There was a wardrobe at the front and everyone was allowed just one hanger.

Sally recalls: 'We also had a cupboard each, which was under the bottom bunks - half the length of the bunk. Anything extra, for example my scrapbooks, I kept under my mattress. I slept in one of the top bunks, so my nose got closer and closer to the roof.'

We had decided to have a name for our bus, which was after all to be our home for two years, and the Evening Post ran a competition. No Bertie the Bus for us (although it would have helped with my children's story).

We considered all the suggestions and chose the title, Sir George White Special, after that pioneer of Bristol transport and British aviation (he founded Bristol Commercial Vehicles and rather more famously the Bristol Aeroplane Company) and founder of local hospitals.

Looking back, I feel it was not a memorable choice (although Dave doesn't agree) but this was the late 60s and we were obviously trying to sound important. These days Bertie would have been a favourite choice. Or something ruder.

The great man's great-grandson, also George White, helped to christen the bus in April, 1970, with a bottle of local cider and the help of the Lord Mayor, Alderman Bert Willcox.

The Lord Mayor with Roger (right) and George White (far right)

Our company title was Omniworld Expo, which looked very impressive on letterheads and reflected our grandiose ideas of selling British goods and particularly toilets - "don't rest on your laurels, buy a British loo" - around the world.

You may recall that Prime Minister Harold Macmillan called our efforts to improve the toilet habits of the world "the wind of change"; although he may have been referring to something else.

The idea was to ship the bus and its assorted chattels from Bristol to Montreal, from where it would be driven to Toronto to pick up most of the group, and then head to the Deep South, the most important target to be in Mexico City in June for the start of the 1970 World Cup.

The bus was due to sail for Montreal on May 3, but a couple of weeks before the shipping company told us that sailing had been brought forward a week.

This meant that preparations were even more hectic and the night before departure everyone worked for 24 hours, all through the night, the girls making the curtains, the men dabbing on paint.

Looking back at the various diaries, you can't escape the conclusion that back in the 1970s men and women were still acutely conscious of the role they were expected to fill, reinforced by education (domestic science v metalwork, needlework v technical drawing).

Of course, we could have worked the other way round, and might well have done so in today's more flexible society, but the fact was that if the men had made the curtains and the women tuned the engine in no time we would have been stuck at the side of a busy highway with the windows covered in nothing but dust.

One early snag, which didn't forbode well for the rest of the trip, was that the bus, much heavier after the conversion than when it was driven onto an area of planking in Mike's garden before the work, became stuck in the mud as we tried to drive it away, and we had to get a heavy tow truck to pull us out!

At noon on May 2 the bus was loaded safely on to a ship at Avonmouth Docks, with Pete travelling on board with it.

The rest of us flew over in two stages - four on May 2, the remainder a week later, including Mike.

He had had a crazed ride behind a rotavator as he tried to tidy up his garden after the bus had left.

He recalls: 'On muddy, claggy and stony ground the machine with four attached tillers is not an easy machine to handle and I have vague memories of the incident, and the cries of 'ride 'em, cowboy' and 'watch out for the coal shed and children's sand pit' from the rest of the crew, as I was dragged through the mud behind this uncontrollable beast.

'My guess that it was then and there that the crew decided that I was banned from driving the bus!

'Roger and Bob noticing my disappointment gave me the new title of "Keeper and repairer of the sparking plug department."

'Being totally mechanically ignorant it took me a little while to realise that there are no sparking plugs in a diesel engine!

'I told them to watch carefully their morning porridge in the future....Lesson one, Don't upset the cook!!.'

Roger was among the first four to arrive in Canada, leaving his bride of nine days, plus Dave and Sally, to stay near Toronto with Sally's parents, who had emigrated several years earlier and were running the Caledon Heath Farm for millionaire Mr C.R.J. Smith. Meanwhile Roger travelled by Greyhound bus to the docks in Montreal, intending to drive the double-decker back to Toronto with Pete, and pick up Bernice, Dave and Sally, before collecting the rest of the group on their arrival at Toronto airport a few days later.

However, he had tremendous difficulty in clearing the bus through Montreal customs.

"I found there was some anti-British feeling in this part of Canada, which is predominantly French/Canadian," he said.

"The fact that the bus was typically English and I spoke very little French aggravated them even more. I was kept waiting for four hours by customs offices, some of whom refused to speak to me in English."

At first the customs officers refused to clear the bus with its examples of British goods and £200 of horse brasses that were to be sold to raise money, even though Roger had money ready to pay custom charges.

Another problem was insurance for the bus. An English broker had assured Roger that insurance would be waiting at the dockside in Montreal. It wasn't. There was just a letter from a Canadian company saying they could not insure the vehicle.

Roger telephoned just about every insurance company and agent in Montreal and none of them would help.

But not all French Canadians were as hostile as those at customs - one insurance agent went out of his way to pick Roger up in his car, and drove him around the city trying to find insurance. He even took him to his home to meet his charming Japanese wife.

Eventually one insurance broker provided temporary cover for 18 days, which would give breathing space for the bus to get to Toronto, and customs cleared the vehicle.

Pete and Roger drove down the King's Highway 401, commonly referred to as Highway 401, to Toronto, a distance of about 400 miles, non-stop all through the night and following day.

Re-united with Bernice, Dave and Sally, they went to the airport to pick up those who had flown in, driving in through the one-way system.

CHAPTER FOUR

Our trip to Toronto, via New York, had been uneventful. My diary recorded: 'Brother Bob took me to Heathrow. Got there by 11.20am and went for a drink; we all missed the call, and got on the plane by the skin of our teeth even though it left an hour late at 2.30pm.

'Saw Newfoundland through window while waiting for the toilet. Temperature 86F in New York we are told. Banked alarmingly as we circled New York, to Mike's horror - he gripped my arm like a vice most of the way. It was my first flight too!

'Cleared customs in two hours and caught the 7.20pm DC9 to Toronto, landing after 100 minutes with a bounce. After drinks in the restaurant with the rest of the team, feeling very nervous, we went to the bus, parked in a nearby car park looking large, red and dependable.'

However, the re-united group soon encountered a problem that was to become a familiar one. 'Sir George', standing a magnificent 14ft 6 inches, came up against a 13ft 6-inch bridge, and though we backed our way along the one-way system, with much waving of red torches, another low bridge brought us to a halt.

My diary recorded: 'The Mounties came to our rescue, in the form of Mountie Reg Chad of the Royal Canadian Mounted Police, who was faced with the dilemma of trying to arrest a double-decker bus (the Mounties always get their bus?) or help us on our way.

'The fact that Roger was a former policeman may have helped - they directed us along a mud road being used in the construction of a nearby flyover, the Mounties blocking traffic until we had completed the manoeuvre, and were soon back on the road.'

As we drove along we were very amused at the interest our bus created, cars slowing down to our speed as they overtook, heads craning, people waving - all very exciting and something that never lost its appeal throughout our travels.

Our destination was the farm run by Sally's parents and we stayed there for several days, learning about living together in a confined space.

On the first day Mike cooked our dinner. It was fish and chips. When it was on the table he gave everyone a shout that it was ready.

Some of us took too long to sit down and the food was cold. Mike gave us a warning: "If you aren't here when I call it will be in the bin." It was a bit like being back at home on the Isle of Wight, late for Mum's Sunday dinner! Anyway, no-one was late again!

We finished doing odd jobs around the bus that we had not had time to complete before we left, earning money working on the farm, and going shop to shop in Toronto selling horse brasses.

My diary recorded: 'It is obvious that we cannot all get up at the same time; there is simply not enough room between the bunks, so we have to do it in stages. Usually it meant lying on your bunk until you hear someone go downstairs, and then quickly getting up before anyone else. We are helped by the fact that some of us like early rising, and others are more reluctant to face the day's challenges. We only have the small sink for washing, which meant that two girls or two fellows (sic) used the kitchen together.

'The toilet is far from comfortable. And it has its funny side, perched on a glistening white throne on the bus rear platform, bumping up and down with the contours of the road, and the terrible thought that if the platform were to break off, as it felt like doing, there I would be sitting on my glass fibre bottom in the middle of a freeway.

'The first day I was sitting there with the bus moving along at a good rate, our driver braked sharply and the sliding door slid back revealing me to the gaze of the usual long queue of interested motorists. With a smile and a wave in the Royal style, I slid the door closed again. The next day I put a lock on it.'

Going to bed usually meant a kick in the ribs for those on the lower bunks as the upstairs tenant climbed up into his narrow perch.

In those early days we only drove occasionally, as the drivers became acquainted with the different conditions.

Roger explained: 'I don't think the camber of the bus was designed for driving on the left, although I could be wrong. I certainly never worried about it tipping, because they are designed to stay upright in the most testing conditions. I think weight was a much bigger problem.

'Remember we had 70 gallons of water up top underneath the Colesies' bed, so we were definitely top heavy.

'Driving the bus was great with the exception that we caused regular accidents as other drivers paid more attention to us than to other vehicles on the road. It was the only time in my life when young women used to hang out of car windows to wave at me. Made you feel like a pop star. Mind you on our one-dollar a day allowance we weren't paid like one. How did we live on that and the communal Backy tin?

'We had a governor on the bus that gave us a max speed of 44mph. Not that that was needed when we climbed mountains in Mexico for days on end at 5mph.

'The worst bit was changing gear and steering. No power steering and after a couple of hours particularly in built-up areas your arms got tired.

'There was no synchromesh on the gearbox so you had to double de-clutch when you changed. When you got it wrong there was a loud crunching of gears and shouts of derision from one's comrades acting as the worst backseat drivers.'

On Sunday, May 10, our first full day at the farm, we relaxed a bit.

But unknown to all of us, a love-bomb was primed and ready to explode. You have to remember that with no email and no mobile phones, it was very difficult to get in touch with someone thousands of miles away, particularly if they were on the move and not able to be contacted by phone.

So whilst back in England, Jan had written a letter to boyfriend Pete, who, as you may recall, had gone with the bus by sea.

Before Bernice left the UK to fly to meet the boys on the bus, Jan – who was coming later with the rest of us – gave the letter to Bern and asked her to give it to Pete.

Bernice forgot to hand it over. It would have been OK had it been a love letter, undying love and all that, but it wasn't. It was a Dear John.

Jan in the kitchen

And that meant when Pete met up with Jan she was not as affectionate as he had hoped she would be. Rather the opposite - Jan would soon be with Bob.

Now, to those who may not know what a Dear John is – the term having fallen out of popular use, made unnecessary by modern ease of communications, particularly social media - it goes back to World War Two when US servicemen serving abroad received letters from home telling them a relationship was over.

In much the same way, the expression 'John Thomas' has fallen out of use; in particular I remember a ex-public schoolboy journalist on the Sunday Times being baffled by the term when we were all reading hot-from-the-press copies of the News of the World in the newsroom at Wapping on a Saturday night many years ago. If anyone doesn't know what it means, see me after.

Anyway, while these tensions were simmering in the background, three men on horseback arrived and had a look around the bus, the first of a stream of people.

We sold some horse brasses and former Horse Guard Don (tall in the saddle), Dave (frail in the saddle) and Joan (fall out of the saddle) went out horse riding.

In the afternoon four of us went fly-fishing in Mr Smith's pond and several rainbow trout showed Canadian hospitality by swimming onto our hooks. Don had a dollar-earning afternoon on a tractor, I fixed up an interview with the Toronto Star and Mr Smith contacted a gift shop proprietor, who promised he would buy some horse brasses. Went to bed at 10pm and I banged my head on the roof. It would be a regular occurrence.

Dave's diary recorded: 'I have developed a very irritating rash on my hands and feet, which later covered most of the body. Sally is giving me some cream, powder and pills so hopefully it will clear soon. We went back into Toronto. Don and I did some shopping. Pete is in bed with a slight temperature.

41

'Don has a cold. It has been all round the crew, but has to be expected when we all live in such a confined space.'

Over the next few days we carried on making the bus fit for purpose, while staying at a garage owned by Dave's uncle at Oakville.

Pete fitted a platform for the spare wheel, Jan and I fitted curtains on the shower, and Dave set up an inside radio. Mosquito nets had been fitted and the shower was working.

We were running out of water too quickly, and as an experiment, and without telling us, Mike made tea out of the water he had used to boil the potatoes. No-one noticed.

Mike had the nickname Ripper, after the Ripper Robots he brought with us to try to market abroad, a big part of the original plan.

We would get a percentage of all the orders. It sounded good in theory, but didn't work out so well. Mike would prove to be a great chef – conjuring up tasty dishes out of the cheapest ingredients.

He was the quartermaster, in charge of the stores. When times were bad, no money in the kitty, he still managed to feed us, no doubt begging and borrowing.

After much struggle, Roger managed to get insurance for 500 dollars from Royal Bank of Canada for the bus to continue its journey.

It was a major achievement because otherwise we would have been forced off the road. In between doing interviews for local papers, I set about cleaning up the putty on the bus windows with Mike's pallet knife, left it in the drawer with putty still on it, and kept my mouth shut when I noticed Mike using it to make his potato pie!

We met several students who told us that when the pollution count hit 30 the authorities started to close the factories, at the 40 level more would close, and when it hit 100 they all closed until it improved.

They reported bad pollution in rivers and lakes, and they no longer swam in Lake Ontario. They blamed the Americans. We went for a walk along the shores of the lake and saw hundreds of dead fish floating in the shallows. They also said that vast areas of corn grow and die because there is no market for it.

Another example of our cruel farming system, where half the world eat too much and the rest are close to starving!

A chap named Bill Hatch came into the garage for petrol, had a look around, examined the toilet and was so impressed he said he would order several for his boats and trailers. It could be our first order.

Another visitor offered us 600 dollars to do a three-day promotion in Winnipeg, but that was hundreds of miles out of our way as we were still planning to be in Mexico City for the World Cup. We turned it down.

Money was, however, very much in our minds. In a letter home on May 18 I said the fact that some members of the group had brought money with them, £80 in one instance (a lot of money in those days!), when others hadn't, had created some tensions.

It was as simple as someone buying a film, chocolate or a Coca-Cola when others couldn't afford to. In one instance there was an inquest into who had drunk out of someone's bottle of orange, left in the fridge. The owner knew some had been "stolen" because he had marked the level of the liquid in the bottle. That was how petty it could become.

On May 21, in a letter to my parents, I said: 'The group had a meeting the other day to sort out some grievances and since then everything has been OK.'

CHAPTER FIVE

So far, the bus had fulfilled the faith we had in it - it grumbled and groaned on uphill gradients, but once over the top the wheels sang and air whistled happily through the windows, even when they were closed.

But no-one seemed to mind the rattles and draughts; it was a minor inconvenience, just as two shavers sharing a sink was difficult, or getting up from bed one person at a time to prevent two people discovering they were trying to get into the same pair of pants (yes, space was that limited!).

We watched people watching us, fish mouths gaping on all sides, unblinking eyes that peer, question and then usually smile. We ate, drank and slept with someone looking over our shoulder. As we bumped along the Freeways cars slowed as they came abreast, motorists waving.

Three girls in a Volkswagen passed, pulled in front and travelled along with us like a dolphin in the bow wave of an old sail boat. There were two of our group in the cab, driver with navigator, who was probably there to help keep him awake.

They laughed at the girls and they mouthed something back. Where we were going? Around the world? They laughed and their eyes promised a lot, but they accelerated away.

"Who was that?" - one of the four girls in our crew had staggered along the lower deck from the kitchen carrying two cups of tea, in soup bowls so it was more difficult to spill and wet the carpet.

We soon had another encounter with a low bridge. Dave was driving on the Queen Elizabeth Highway towards Niagara Falls and as we approached the Stony Creek junction we slowed as usual to see how low the bridge ahead was, and it said 13ft 9in.

Dave stopped and then cautiously drove forward as Don at the back signalled to the traffic to slow down - they were passing us at speed on both sides!

We were obviously about two inches too high and were in the process of letting the tyres down in the hope that this would enable us the scrape under, when the police arrived.

They stopped all the traffic as we crept forward, having moved over to the middle lanes where the bridge was highest, and scraped underneath.

After getting air for the tyres at the next garage, we drove seven miles along a service road to Grimsby, which proved to be the most friendly place we had visited yet - people clapped as we passed, and one English exile burst into tears!

My diary recorded: 'Trouble with engine, noisy gear changes. Bought more than 26 dollars of grub - we haven't eaten today except for bread at breakfast, and it's nearly 8pm! Trying to repair bus, or see what is wrong, while on the move, peering through open hatch in floor. Clutch adjusted - there was too much free play in it.'

We were soon able to see and hear the Niagara Falls from across the river. I wrote: 'It was a gorgeous view, everyone very impressed, except for Ripper who, after looking at the Fall, proclaimed 'Just like Snuff Mills' (a small river and waterfall in Bristol).

They put on the lights, colours changing, as we arrived. Vera Lynn was on the radio singing softly 'When I grow too old to dream', very nostalgic, with the falls pounding and the lights flickering through the bus windows.'

I also reported a 'bit of friction on the bus', but eight of us went off to have a drink in a so-called English pub (which didn't have any English beer) and a game of darts, with a hot dog as a main meal, and we were back at the bus in our bunks by 12.30am.

Next morning I woke up with water in my hair, and a constant drip, drip from the roof, obviously a result of damage caused when the bus scraped under a bridge. My mattress was soaked and I went downstairs and slept on the floor, to be woken very early by a policeman who told us to move on.

My diary continues: 'Don drove and I navigated to Niagara in the Lake. We parked in a quiet spot next to the lake at 7.20am, outside a mansion flying the Union Jack. Mike burnt the bacon.

'I went into the toilet, dropped my pants, found the toilet roll was wet through, soggy bottom, pulled up my pants; they were soaked, soggy pants! Not a good start to the day. It gets worse - Roger and Bern had a close look at our finances, it didn't take long, we have just 12 dollars left!'

Sally was kept busy looking after invalids, mostly colds and sore throats, as well as doing her regular early morning clean up downstairs while the rest of us were asleep. She always had boundless energy.

Among people who saw us parked up and stopped for a chat was a public health inspector, formerly from Swansea, who said that the houses along the river flew Union Jacks for two reasons - to show the flag to the Americans on the other side of the river, and because many of them were connected to the Empire Loyalists organisation, who originally leased this area of land.

Later, we saw a figure in tight blue flared jeans gesticulating from the doorway of the nearby mansion, and Don wandered up to see him, followed by the rest of us.

We were invited in for drinks; the four men who lived there wanted to learn more about our trip.

Two were in dressing gowns, and they were quite openly gay - in fact one said to Bob "only two beds to make up." Bob smiled nervously. The dog, a male, became quite affectionate with Don. The house was most luxurious, all silver cups, thick carpets and pianos.

'A most beautiful house,' my diary recorded, 'dark wood panelling, easy chairs that were as relaxing as a sleeping pill, huge cooker and freezer, numerous paintings and statues.'

They bought 50 dollars' worth of horse brasses and proved most hospitable. The drink flowed. Our host - who looked like Julius Caesar - was a leading eye specialist, who loved antiques. He normally lived alone.

The chap in the flairs was the Director of the National Housing Research Council. He said the flag was there because all the locals disliked the new Maple Leaf flag, so they sported the Union Jack at every occasion.

Don nipped into the toilet and returned with the verdict: "It was a beautiful clear-out, a double exit throne, the first I've seen."

We all shook hands when we left and Don, Mike and I got a double handshake, which, in those days (when we Brits were not used to gay people being so up front about it) we found slightly worrying.

We drove into the nearby town, Niagara on the Lake. which was the first capital of Upper Canada - the first Parliament held here in 1792. Around the town people grew grapes, peaches, cherries, pears and plums.

Roger, Bernice and Mike visited the gift shop, selling a few items, while Dave and I visited the local newspaper, the Niagara Advance.

They put us in touch with the organisers of the Virgil Stampede, the second biggest rodeo/horseshoe in Canada, and we agreed to attend the next day and conduct a two-day sale from the bus. Pete repaired a gasket leak. We had fried chicken and mash for dinner at about 10pm, and I finished the day with a wonderful hot shower.

Overnight there was a thunderstorm – 'I couldn't hear the thunder because of Roger's snoring,' my diary recorded.

Now I want to break away from the nuts and bolts and even gaskets of the trip and talk about something a lot more interesting – sex.

I have briefly mentioned one or two distractions during my early life, including the girls of a private school, some of who made St Trinian's seem like a nunnery.

I think I must mention here that to get to Bembridge I used to steal my parent's car, after sneaking out of the kitchen window of their house in Sandown, and once became stuck in the mud on the Downs with a young lady from Ayr, who turned out to have the most inaccessible underwear since the Vestal Virgins.

That is not really relevant, apart from the fact that I did briefly consider asking her to remove her iron bra so that I could attempt to get purchase under the wheels with it.

As it happened we slid down the hill and I bent the exhaust, which I later blamed on my younger brother, so no harm done. As a matter of interest, I learned only recently that at the very moment I was stealing out of the rear window, my elder brother was slipping out of the window at the front en route to his own midnight encounters, though I never saw him at Bembridge and I had the car anyway, so hard luck.

Anyway back to the sex. We the bus crew never embarked upon this adventure with any idea of seducing huge numbers of the population of the States and Central and South America – in fact, as previously mentioned, there were amongst the 11 of us three couples, who had their hands full already so to speak, although I must say they carried it off most discreetly with no yelps or shrieks and hardly a rattle.

Did they do it? They must have, but mostly when the rest of us were out, or busy downstairs driving the bus. Making love on the upper deck of a moving bus? Just hold on tight and enjoy the ride! It probably beats the Mile High Club any time.

You have to remember that this was 1970, and British bands had been making a huge impact on American youth for the past ten years.

Bruce Springsteen, who would have been 21 when we started our trip, recalls he and his friends tried to cultivate an English accent to attract the girls after watching the Dave Clark Five tour the USA in 1965.

Young American women were obviously fascinated by our accent (even the Bristol version!), so it wasn't that long before some of us were making good friends and 'cementing' international relations, although at the time to vigorous young men and woman it seemed like ages.

More of that later. Right now, back to the gaskets and horse brasses.

We were full of optimism as we parked the bus at the showground. The weather was improving, and there were lots of farming people in their best suits.

However, a fairground worker's observation that Virgil was a "two-bit town" seemed to be realised when we sold just two horse brasses all morning. Rain ended our efforts, and after cheese pie for lunch we had a brandy/coffee to restore sagging spirits.

Later, Doug Evans from the Advance took us to the English Club at St Catherine's; we parked the bus outside, set up two tables selling brasses and sold $80 worth in no time! Most of the English exiles had lost their accent and drawled, though Scottish always fought its way through.

One chap told me he used to drive London buses, and another was a bus mechanic working on the ten double-deckers they had at Niagara Falls. He was drunk.

To avoid him, Mike and I took the brasses back into the bus, where Dave was showing lots of enthusiastic people around. I took charge of two girls wearing 'traditional' English gear - white floppy hats and rose-decorated dresses.

You wouldn't have seen that around Bristol - Henley Regatta perhaps - not Bristol. Some of the blokes we were later to meet in San Francisco would have killed to wear clothes like that. I was stunned on one occasion when a chap came up to me and asked if he could take my trousers off - they were tweed flares and he wanted to buy them!

My diary recorded: 'Roger made a good speech which was wildly applauded. We must seek out more of these types of clubs, because often the people either collect horse brasses or had to leave them back home in England. Emptied toilet.'

Next day, Sunday May 17, we drove 16 miles to Niagara Falls, guided by the bus mechanic (now sober), and met Norman Watson, who owned the fleet of ten buses that for the past five years had carried passengers around the Falls at a price of $3.50c for a day ticket. Each bus had a hostess.

'After a visit to Marineland where porpoises leapt huge distances and alligators eyed us hungrily, we set off on a bus tour.

'The Falls look astonishingly close, rolling, green and menacing, whilst at a distance the spray is like a white veil and rocks jut up like a toothy grin. Some of the group with money to spare went on a cable car across the river,' my diary recorded.

In the evening we returned to the site of the Stampede, ready for selling brasses the following day. It was Mike's day off from cooking, so 'someone made a sort of mince beef stew, which together with perfumed tea and iced apples played havoc with our digestive systems.'

Don and I woke the crew up next morning with the bus horn. We set the tables up outside but none of the locals was very interested. We even tried giving a free tour of the bus with every sale, but no-takers.

We sold just $27 worth all day. Luckily, finances had improved; we had about $215 left. However, the mood on the bus was depressing; most people wouldn't get up, so we didn't have any breakfast, and we lost two hours cleaning, planning time. We had to go to the Immigration Department and extend our stay.

'We have to sell all our goods before we can leave Canada, but we spend half the time sitting around waiting,' I recorded.

That day Pete and Sally sold £36 of horse brasses at Niagara Falls, and I (Roger, Dave and I all smoked pipes when we could afford the baccy) made a pipe rack!

We didn't have time for lunch, we extended our permit until June 19 and Mike bought a chip pan, so chips tonight! We had a meeting and resolved that everyone would get up earlier.

The next morning everyone was up by 7am and we were ready to leave at 7.15am. That's the way to do it!

Over the next two days we tried to sell our horse brasses in Ontario. I walked for 10 hours carrying suitcases, going from shop to shop, without much luck, but on the second day as Bern and I walked miserably back with aching feet along Yong Street - which at that time claimed to be the longest street in the world - having sold just £13 worth, we called in at Drake's Antiques, and a Mr Munn, an Englishman, promised a big order. True to his word the next day he bought $224 worth.

Mike, Sally, Pete and Bob had also been selling brasses, while Roger and Jan were talking to potential clients about selling ad space on the side of the bus. They were ideally suited to ad sales – Roger a born negotiator, Jan with a winning smile.

We had two more encounters with low objects. First we knocked down a power line overhanging the entrance to a car park, which angered the attendant, and then we had a second saga at Stony Creek - we went the wrong way up Highway 20 and ended up at the bridge that had caused us so much trouble before.

This time, however, we went up a lane the wrong way and managed to get through "by about the width of Pete's moustache."

We also came to the attention of the Mounties again. Constable Robert Shaw stopped us and questioned our size and permits, apparently at first thinking we were one of the double-deckers from Niagara Falls hijacked by a maniac.

He was very friendly when he discovered the truth and led us to a great parking spot next to the lake, where two other officers joined us. They were shown around the bus and, while they were having a cuppa with us, a brand new Mustang floated slowly past, the driver leaning out to shout "Dig that crazy trailer" with which he crashed into a white fence! The police officers checked him out before he drove off, the front of his car looking worse for wear.

In a letter home I said: 'It's now Friday morning (May 22) and four of us are up. A typical day starts at 7.30am with Mike and Don bringing tea round to everyone. Then we have cornflakes and tea.'

We were preparing for our crossing into the USA. Much useful work had been done to prepare the bus since we arrived at Toronto, and we had sold many of our horse brasses and raised much-needed funds.

We had also enjoyed the social life and made many friends. But now would come the serious bit - the start of our travels to the World Cup finals in Mexico City in just a few weeks' time.

We made one final effort to get rid of our horse brasses, selling on the streets and in a pub at Niagara Falls, making more than $400. We also brought down some overhead electric cables passing through Hamilton; Bernice said it was like a firework display.

'We took part in a parade of buses at Niagara. Overfilled the water tank and flushed Sally down the back stairs. Toilet wet through again,' said the diary.

After a final farewell at the English Club, with Pete driving, we crossed into the USA at Lewiston Bridge, near Queenstown. Customs took just 20 minutes.

It was Sunday May 24. My diary recorded: 'We stopped at Buffalo, on a university campus, at about 5.30am. Feels a bit alien here, I don't know why. We enjoyed Canada.'

We were entering the United States at a difficult time - the height of the Vietnam War protests. Just three weeks earlier at Kent State University in Ohio members of the Ohio National Guard fired 67 rounds over a period of 13 seconds, killing four students and wounding nine others, one of whom suffered permanent paralysis.

Some of the students who were shot had been protesting against the American invasion of Cambodia, which President Richard Nixon announced in a television address on April 30. However, other students who were shot had merely been walking nearby or observing the protest from a distance.

The car park upon which we rested had been the scene of a student riot the previous weekend, when 1,000 police and soldiers with tanks faced down students, who were protesting about the killing of the Kent State University students.

We went to a garage for diesel, at a cost of 28 cents a gallon (2s4p old money) and took on 28 gallons. We topped up the batteries with water - they stopped using distilled water over there years ago.

We were invited to stay the night at the garage and did so. It was run by two brothers, both of who enlisted and fought in Vietnam from the age of 17. They hated it. Jim used to patch up crashed helicopters. He repaired 240 in two years.

His brother married a Vietnamese girl. Their mother said she lived on sedatives while they were away.

On Sunday May 24, 1970, we woke up in the car park at the University of Buffalo. Wet and dreary weather in what looks like a drab area. Several students stopped by and had a chat. All thought it a fab idea and wished us luck. A film producer from CBC also came along and said he might look us up later on the trip. We later drove to a shopping centre for food and fuel.

It was then that the simmering tensions over the love triangle on the bus exploded. Whilst at the diesel pump Pete wandered off without telling anybody. When he didn't come back a search was organised. Roger and Mike went to the police station to report him missing.

For several days we had been concerned that there was friction between Pete and Jan, that they were no longer a couple, and, yes, we had noticed that she had become close (yep, really close) to Bob. You can't really fail to notice such problems in a small group, living so closely together as we were.

A police car pulled in to say Pete had collapsed on a local highway and was in hospital. After a couple of hours he was released and came back to the bus and was put to bed. We had a meeting to discuss the incident.

Pete had also not been well recently, and as a result of all these pressures had become depressed and irritable. It was felt Pete might have to leave the bus at New York and return home.

CHAPTER SIX

We were just a week away from the start of the World Cup (May 31) in Mexico. Realistically, we had no chance of getting there for the 1st round matches, but we were determined to see England, the cup holders, play, and confident that they would do well enough to reach the quarter finals.

We had sacrificed an offer of a $800 promotion and advertising work in Canada to continue our journey, and were hopeful that we would quickly attract enough attention to get similar work in the United States and earn the money we needed to carry on.

First we had to get out of Buffalo! We were surrounded by low bridges and finally scraped through after letting down the tyres once again. It took paint off the roof.

Unfortunately it brought us to the attention of the police, who escorted us to a police station 50 yards away and after some debate about whether they should detain us for not having the right permit they became very friendly and their Chief, Benedict L Kostrzewski (a Pole, like many other officers) invited us to stay there to make minor repairs and, of course, reflate the tyres. He said he wouldn't arrest us; we could regard ourselves as his "guests".

Because of all the low bridges, the police arranged for the Department of Transport to organise a route for us, and we stayed overnight to give them the time to do it.

Pete, Mike and I walked down to a supermarket next morning, and as we walked back a police car pulled up and gave us a lift back!

We met Gary Stranges of the Buffalo Evening News, who said the state had made it an offence to call police pigs, and that they were treating us so well because we were a bit odd and needed help.

He said it was a country for machines, not people; there were no pavements, everyone drove, no-one walked. The Police Captain later took the girls down to a launderette, and that evening Officer Dynowski was given the duty of looking after us for an evening at a local bar, Gilligans, with draft beer and Singapore Slims, all free.

The permit we had obtained made clear that we were only to travel on the designated route, all State roads, and if we ventured off it we would have to get separate permission from the "proper authorities".

The following day we set off at 7.10am. My diary read: 'We headed along the planners' route. There are little red and white-topped fire hydrants lurking in the hedgerows, like officious little policemen. Stopped by a State policeman, who looked a bit stern at first, but soon cheered up and was very friendly. He got on his radio and as a result we had a police escort from Greece as far as Webster.

First it was a police car, then a car and motor-cycle, and then two motor-cycles. They held up traffic for us as we went through Rochester. We were all very amused, and the cop was showing off a bit on his bike.'

We travelled off the main highway because of the bridges and covered 207 miles, our best day yet, once reaching a record 50mph (Dave disputes this, saying we would have been unable to reach that speed "even if we fell off a mountain"), before stopping at 6.45pm.

Soon afterwards a young chap on a bike told us we could park on his grand pappy's cornfield, which we did. After dinner of cottage pie (gorgeous) and sherbet ice cream (horrible) the young chap took us fishing and apparently poaching, as we had to get across someone's front garden, a stream and a barbed wire fence, for just one large frog, which we think was dead anyway. The scenery was lovely, lakes and small hills, I recorded, and not many people.

The following day we turned off at Duanesburg to visit a police HQ and get a route through Albany, but when Don started up to leave the bus sank down to its chassis in loose earth.

Luckily there was an excavator nearby that pulled us out. We had another police escort to get to Albany - at one point the cop forced an oncoming car with women passengers off the road so we could get through! On the Friday we arrived at Red Hook fairly early and the police arranged for us to park at a local school and took Joan and Bernice to the launderette.

'It is the best scenery we have seen around here, huge areas of trees, greens and browns, and sometimes rocky banks at the side of the roads,' I recorded. 'Rex Maine (Chief of Police) gave us some police badges and bread, and we put on hats to publicise Steckler's Foods. Mr Steckler said he had seen us in a photo in the New York Times.

'We developed a diesel leak and stopped at a garage in the village, and they repaired it for us and gave us free fuel. We had free meat from Mr Steckler and free milk and bread from the local bakery. What hospitality!'

I added: 'Kids think that we know the Beatles, and that I am an Indian! (I must have been trying out my Welsh accent on them).'

We reached Peekskill and were taken to police HQ. It was Friday, May 29, just two days before the World Cup started, and we were still over two thousand miles away and yet to sort out a permit to travel on through New York State.

I want to dwell for a moment on the subject of football. It was never a driving (!) passion to get to the World Cup on time, as Roger has previously mentioned.

In fact, I doubt whether the girls were interested at all; it was just a stop en route to the fruit fields of California, where we hoped to make enough money to pay for the next part of the trip.

In those days soccer was even more of a male sport than it is now.

I was a Portsmouth supporter until I moved away from the Isle of Wight, then a Gillingham fan because I covered their games home and away for the Kent Evening Post – even after manager Basil Hayward banned me from the dressing room for calling the team hippopotamuses (I couldn't spell it in those days). He told me I was a word I can spell, but choose not to.

I was never a Bristol City or Rovers fan. In the last two seasons (as I wrote this) I have once again learned to enjoy soccer live, a season ticket holder at Derby County matches, and it is very gratifying to see the change towards family crowds, with lots of mums and kids, instead of the yobs of the past.

It may be interesting to note that my knees are not as flexible as when I was scaling those orange tree ladders 40 years ago, so that when Derby score (infrequently) and all the supporters leap to their feet in salutation, I struggle to keep up; so much so that by the time I have risen, arms outstretched in triumph they are back in their seats and I stand there on my own feeling a bit of an idiot.

I must share one story – we had a photographer at the Sheffield Star, who covered soccer matches on rainy Saturday afternoons.

One particularly cold, wet day he was watching Sheffield Wednesday play at Hillsborough and at half time he changed ends to get behind the goal the Owls were attacking, knelt down, and was then stricken by the need to have a pee.

Unable to leave his post (!) and assured by the fact that he was wearing a large cape that would hide what he was up to from the crowd, he decided to relieve himself on the ground, which he did.

At once there arose a mighty din from the fans behind him, akin to the sort of applause that met a wonder goal from David Hirst, and, perplexed because he would certainly have never have missed a Hirsty thunderbolt, he half turned to see what was going on behind him and discovered that huge clouds of steam were billowing from under the edge of the cape!

I will always remain a Shanklin FC supporter, and that's because I covered their matches for the Isle of Wight Guardian for several seasons.

I still remember how cold it was on the County Ground, standing making notes, warming my hands on my pipe, the only spectator. They were pretty dreadful and only attracted a crowd of more than a dozen for cup ties.

The referee made himself unpopular on one occasion, was shouted off the pitch and, as he closed the wooden door to his room, an arrow thudded into it and stuck, quivering. It was quite rural there at times.

If the Blues were short of a linesman, I sometimes pocketed my notepad and walked the line, and once when times were particularly hard I borrowed a pair of black shorts and turned out for them at inside left.

I was wearing a brown shirt. I threatened a lot but didn't do much. Half way through the first half I tackled one of the Brading players and he said: "What are you doing, ref?"

On another occasion when they played Ryde Sports (a good team) in the cup, I had told the manager, Derek Wheeler, that my brother, Tony, played a bit of football and he promptly selected him at inside right. Within a minute someone passed Tony the ball and he rammed it (well, knee-capped it) into the net. "This boy's great!" shouted Derek, clapping me on the back. They lost 13-1.

So that's my soccer pedigree, and not very impressive. But I was a keen England fan and still hoped to get to the World Cup in time to see them play.

Anyway, while we waited to sort out our permit the New York State police allowed us to stay in their yard, next to an obviously polluted stretch of lake.

It was an area for poor whites, most of them squatters, with chickens and dogs everywhere and wooden shacks built on piles on the lakeshore. The atmosphere was not pleasant and the cops were jumpy.

However, our spirits improved when a nationalised American, Scot Stuart Cummings, turned up and said we could park at his residence on Bear Mountain - the Oldstone Inn, a beautiful house in grounds overlooking the Hudson River. A sample of menu prices in his restaurant: roast rib of beef was $6.25c or £2.12s (£2.60 new money); curried rice and chicken $6, haggis $2 (85p).

My diary recorded that Pete was ill and the fridge had packed in, meaning our milk was off. Hopefully, the two were not related.

The next day we had business in New York, permits and horse brasses business, so all of us except Pete borrowed a Jeep (it must have been a big one!) and drove in, meeting heavy traffic.

The temperature was in the 80s and our first impression was of a filthy city, with pretty but unfriendly girls and lots of scowling faces. My diary recorded that breakfast (hash browns, egg, toast, coffee and orange) cost today's equivalent of 38p.

We went to a building on 5th Avenue to see someone about buying horse brasses, but discovered it had just been evacuated because of a bomb scare.

From there we visited the Consular General's office on 3rd Avenue, and were re-directed to the Trade office about four blocks away. Dave and Roger went in to discuss permits, while the rest of us admired the office girls as we waited patiently in the foyer. I presume our girls must have been elsewhere.

We were told the Consul had been in touch with Mexico about our trip, and also with British officials in Houston. Dave and I then went to the Mexico Tourist Office to see about a route, and the chap there soon marked a route on a map with a big green pencil, but he added that he didn't know how tall the bridges were!

The rest of our group had been back to see the people who could fly in some more horse brasses, but they were told we would not be able to pick them up for 48 hours, nor would be able to get any credit! So we left without the brasses and with no permit - not a very successful day.

We saw a young lad, aged about 12, fire a revolver into the ground, and two women, who were passing, grabbed him and roughed him up. We were glad to jump into Stuart's swimming pool when we got back, just before discovering that the front nearside wheel of the Jeep had almost come off!

As usual, the local people were very hospitable, particularly those who had emigrated from Britain. One, Derek Tudor, a cop, originally from Shrewsbury, took us to his home for a drink and a barbecue.

We stayed at the Oldstone Inn for three days while Dave went to Poughkeepsie to try to get a permit (he succeeded), and Roger, Don and Bob worked on the engine.

I talked to some newspapers. In a letter home I said: 'We are also waiting for one of the girls to have a hospital check-up - guess why? Let's hope she isn't, and if she is I can state without fear of contraception (an old Hylda Baker joke) that it wasn't me!'

I added: 'It's funny living like this, we don't even think about what it used to be like, working every day – it's a billion miles away. I feel homesick sometimes. But we are in good spirits and will be picking up some more horse brasses soon.'

Dave was in charge of navigation. On Tuesday 2 June 1970 his diary recorded: 'I went off to Poughkeepsie in a borrowed vehicle to try and sort out a route.

'A few of us pored over maps looking at routes and then other maps and information checking out the height of bridges.

'We finally found a circuitous route into New Jersey, but they have no idea what the roads are like there. The main problem is that the North East coast is criss-crossed with railways and the original bridges were suitable for the time.

'When I got back in the car and tried to start it there was a horrible noise. Found that the starter motor was hanging off. I got filthy fixing it. Back at the bus most of the crew had gone off with Fred and Joyce to Connecticut. Joan had stayed behind to do some washing, so she did my dirty clothes straight away.'

On Thursday, June 4, we left the Oldstone Inn en route to Mexico.

It was a big day, but we still had time to think of our stomachs, stopping to pick some fruit and vegetables; potatoes were $3 for 50 pounds, or 6d a pound old money.

We crossed over the River Delaware and made good time on the 209. We stopped in the early evening and emptied the toilet (quite a ceremony this, with two carrying the shiny white container, one watching for snakes, and another with a huge shovel with which to dig a hole).

We reflected on a good day, but although we had covered 140 miles of quiet roads and lovely countryside (apart from the mosquitoes) Dave worked out that, in fact, we had as the crow flies only travelled 60 miles because of avoiding low bridges.

I noted that I hadn't showered for three days, and I was a bit tired of being nice to people, who wanted to look inside the bus. We had smashed three unbreakable plates that day and resolved to check that everything in the kitchen was secure before we started off next day.

We had some sympathy with a truck carrying another truck that was stuck under a bridge near Carlisle, PA, and they were letting the tyres down.

There were lots of bridges as we headed along Route 81 towards Bristol, Virginia, and my diary noted that we hit one before lunch, and another shortly after, but little damage to the bus, which was what mattered!

The drivers were getting more confident, and I counted that we passed under six bridges in six miles without slowing much at all.

The Shenandoah Mountains were a long row of dark hills, with clouds beneath their summits 'like lace on a row of black cushions.'

We covered over 350 miles, passing under (or scraping) 150 bridges, that day, and my diary recorded: 'We got through two Union Jacks on our flagpole today, so Jan is busy sewing a huge new one.'

The next day Roger, Mike and Don were up early and started the bus up and moved out. The route held well apart from one small diversion.

Just after completing it we were again stopped by a State Trooper. He hinted at the need for special permits to travel and we avoided a direct reply as we haven't got one.

We told him all about the trip and Roger showed him his International Police Association card.

In the end his parting remark was: "Far be it for me to get involved in international relations over our trivial traffic regulations for the sake of a few feet of bus." We offered him a cup of tea but he declined and we carried on our way.

The following day (Saturday, June 6th) we started again at 7am with the new flag flying 'proudly, and cutting our speed by half!'

I phoned the Bristol Herald Courier and told them we, a bus and crew from Bristol, England, were on our way, and we arrived at 2.30pm having already travelled 250 miles that day (which must have been a new record) and parked outside the newspaper office in Peer Street.

Bristol is split into two by the state border (which runs down the middle of the street) with, at that time, 5,000 people living on the Virginia side and 25,000 on the Tennessee side. We were told that if a fugitive from one side crosses over, the other side have to apply for an extradition treaty (it may not have been true).

There were two mayors and two administrative offices and each side had its own schools. "It's as if we are 100 miles apart," said Mayor Red Littleton (Virginia side).

Mayor Littleton wrote to Bernice's father, Bert, who coincidentally was to become Lord Mayor of Bristol, England, a few years later, saying he had met us and that we were being well looked after by our twin city.

The other Mayor, Gerry King, met us at the newspaper office and arranged for us to park at the Silver Creek Park, and we had a police escort there. We were guests of the town and able to use the showers and toilet free, and were taken fishing that evening, and the following day taken to a drag race meeting, the Spring Nationals, which had been attended by 30,000 people the previous day.

It was there that we realised just what petrol-heads the Americans were a long time before Clarkson hit our TV screens.

A drag car called the "Green Monster" powered by an aircraft jet engine was at the other end of the drag track with its parachutes deployed to stop it racing off before it had left the start line!

They invited us to drive the bus to the start line alongside the green machine. Unfortunately we could not get under the access, because we were too high.

In the evening, as we headed on foot for a fish and chip shop, a motor-cycle cop caught us up and took us there 'a police escort for fish and chips – neat,' I recorded. The local paper had featured us prominently, but once again had described us as "students". We were also entertained to tea by the English Ladies Group.

We seemed a world away from Mexico City, but somehow found out about the unfounded shoplifting allegation against England captain Bobby Moore, and then learned that England had won their first match, 1-0 against Romania, on June 2, which cheered us considerably. The last thing we wanted to happen was to get to Mexico City and discover that England had been knocked out.

In today's world of quick and easy communication, with mobile phones that can put you in contact with someone on another continent as easy as if you were ringing the chip shop down the road, it is difficult to visualise how cut off from our previous lives we were in those days.

Ringing home cost money, and it was difficult to go into a call box with enough coins to pay the bill! You would have needed a bucket. And as soccer was not a big sport in the USA, the World Cup did not feature in many newspapers.

We had no television, and only American (or Mexican) stations on the radio (we couldn't understand them). Internet and emails were the stuff of science fiction. So we were often out of touch with England's progress.

It may be interesting to note here that the first hand-held mobile phone was demonstrated by Dr Martin Cooper of Motorola in 1973, using a handset weighing around 1 kg. That was a year after we came back to England at the end of our trip. In 1983, the DynaTAC 8000x was the first to be commercially available.

Anyway, back to our travels. On Monday, June 8, we left Bristol and headed south, the weather getting hotter, the grass browner. We saw few police, and had to make a 30-mile detour to avoid a low bridge.

The bus was going well and diesel was getting cheaper, down to 25 cents a gallon. We saw a cowboy riding along the road. We stopped after 14 hours on the road, 30 miles short of Birmingham, Alabama, and still over 1,000 miles short of our target.

The next day we needed to get to New Orleans if we were to have any chance of reaching Mexico on time, but we started late because Sally's alarm didn't go off (which shows how much we depended on her getting us up!). We had trouble with a few bridges in Birmingham, and were helped by patrolman Ted Trammel, who led us out of town.

His sergeant said we would find Southern police much friendlier than their Northern counterparts. We encountered more low bridges and had to hold traffic up while we cautiously negotiated one.

My diary read: 'Poor shacks with blacks outside in Birmingham, and queues of blacks lining up for jobs. It is 10 to 2 and we still have 210 miles to go.'

We did it, stopping at 9.30pm on the West side of New Orleans, next to a swamp. The air was full of mosquitoes in a mist so thick that we couldn't see where we were going and so we decided to pull over for the night. We made sure the windows and doors were all closed, the mosquito blinds pulled and Mike had got the dinner on.

We were all sitting down eating and listening to the mossies outside when we heard a train in the distance. It got a little louder, then a little louder still everyone carried on eating. It was Mike, who was the first to put his knife and fork down, followed one by one by the rest of us. The train was now very near.

Talk about 'rabbits caught in headlights'. We were all glued to our seats convinced that we were parked on the line! A huge whoosh as the train went by - it turned out that we had parked no further than six feet from the line at the side of a level crossing!

We were up at 4am for an early start, and it was surprisingly busy on the roads. We soon encountered a series of low bridges, mostly 14ft 6 inches clearance, which gave us little room to make a mistake. Several were major bridges spanning rivers, including Long Allen Bridge over the River Atchafalaya, where there were 20 low spans, which we just cleared.

At Houston, Texas, we picked up a police escort, two motor-cycle cops, riding behind and in front, forcing the traffic to give way, even at red lights. We stayed the night at the central police station, and it was there that Roger heard the dismal news that three days earlier Brazil had beaten England 1-0.

This was billed as the unofficial world championship - England, the holders, against Brazil, the favourites. The match is best remembered for a Pelé near-miss.

His powerful close-range downward header was kept out by an amazing save from Gordon Banks, who somehow managed to get down to the ball and flick it upwards and over the bar.

In the end, a single Jairzinho goal was enough to win the game for Brazil. My diary does not record how we felt about this, but it would have been a big disappointment. We had another chance to get through to the quarter-finals, a match against the Czechs on June 11.

The police took several of us to a launderette in a poor part of downtown Houston. Their last words to us were: "Don't leave on your own, wait for us, it's not very safe around here."

We had finished the washing and were waiting around when we heard what we thought was a car backfiring outside. Moments later the door was flung open and a little old lady, who turns out to be the mother of the guy running the launderette, came rushing through the door and marches up to her son and said in a matter of fact voice: "Son, you'll never guess what's just happened!"

"No, Ma, what's that?" the launderette manager said.

The little old lady still walking towards her son went on: "I was walking down the street when this car comes down the road, some guy winds down a window, points a gun at me and shoots. I tell you, son, if it happens again I'm gonna call the cops."

"Yea, I think I would as well, Ma," said her son getting on with his work.

We were glad when the police came back and took us out of there.

Roger discovered that we didn't have a casing for the thermostat, which would have stopped the engine boiling over in Mexico. It was quite a blow, as was the fact that we couldn't scrounge a shower.

So we borrowed a hose and washed down the bus and ourselves (in our cossies), which was really refreshing, even though it was 11.30pm (81degreesF).

We were warned not to walk around the city, and, as we had discovered elsewhere, the white cops had a poor view of black people. "They have criminal minds, they should live with their own sort," said one. It was, and still is, totally racist and maybe we should have said so, but at the time it seemed the wrong time and place. My diary recorded: 'Ripper, all in white, looks like the wild colonial boy.'

There were 350 murders in Houston the previous year, including five police officers. Pete was shown the results of a shotgun blast that killed a 14-year-old boy in a car, and was sick. The police laughed about it. Two million people lived there, yet there were less police than Bristol, which had a quarter of that population.

The police helped us repair our fridge, which had not been working for several days. We had been discussing how to cool the bus inside, but we had no air conditioning unit and no other ideas.

However, next day, it became a bit cooler as we headed down Route 59 to Beeville, where we stopped at the Trading Post, Blueberry Hill, to see if we could sell some brasses.

The owner, Raymond Eissler, gave us free cool drinks and phoned up millionaire Mr Littlejohn, who had an English wife, and they came and had a look.

Mr Eissler offered us a horned Mexican toad, said to spit blood, but we declined. It was near here that some of the crew were taken rattlesnake hunting with a guy, who used a crossbow.

He did this not to damage the skin, which he sold. The meat was eaten and according to those that tasted it, it was a real delicacy. Certainly better than the grey squirrel that Mike cooked one night when money was low and we were desperate. I don't remember now how it tasted, but I bet the nuts were crunchy

It was arranged that we visit Chase Field, the local naval air station, one of only two in the USA. We drove into a hangar, where men were working on two F9 Cougar trainers, and all work stopped as we parked the bus next to them. They gathered round and we had some interesting conversation.

There were nearly 3,000 men and women on the station, which had 2,000 operations a day. We went to the control tower and the weather station. The met man said there were tornadoes further north, and he had seen a tornado pick up a locomotive and carry it five miles.

It was a cooler day, but Mr Eissler warned us that Laredo - where we were heading - was the hottest place he had been. He gave us an ice-box, which was very welcome.

Friday, June 12, was our last day in Texas, as we planned to cross into Mexico. We started at 9am and made slow progress, having to stop to arrange insurance for Mexico.

We drove on through scrubland, 50 miles without a building, buzzards and a dead skunk on the road. A few cattle wandered through the cactus and bushes.

We reached Laredo and there were far more Mexicans on the US side than Americans. The temperature was 104 degrees. Roger crossed the bridge over the river to speak to Mexican customs, but they refused to talk to him, turning their backs, because of his long hair.

So Roger and I had emergency haircuts and Pete trimmed his beard.

CHAPTER SEVEN

We started across at 4.30pm, and although the border guard at first told us to go back he became more helpful when he heard the embassy had made the arrangements. We got through the check-points at about 7.30pm (still 340 miles to go to Mexico City) and caused a lot of interest from local people. Some obviously knew the England chant!

There were kids everywhere trying to sell drinks and gum. My diary recorded: 'Poverty stricken areas, little wooden shacks packed with people. How different from the US side! We stopped in the outskirts of the town to buy watermelons from some men on a lorry - we knocked them down from ten dollars to one dollar for two-and-a-half melons. They must think we are stupid!' (We did well - a melon cost 5 dollars back in Peekskill).

We discovered our water was off, tasting bad, although we had filled up that day, so we used a water purifier for the first time.

We were a bit confused about the time, not knowing if we had gained another hour - anyway, at 8.15pm or 9.15pm it was dark.

With the bus radiator in danger of boiling over, we stopped off the 85 and parked near a cafe, with several trucks outside. Dave and I went in and had a chat in broken English with a Mexican, who was a Brazil fan. We bought a beer (it was better than the water in the bus!) and annoyed the proprietor by sitting on a table, which was, of course, bad manners. I have always felt bad about that.

Back at the bus we introduced our rota guard system: 11pm to 2am and 2am to 5am, one driver staying in bed all night for an early start, Don, on this occasion.

We were off early next morning (Saturday, June 13) and soon made Monterey, where we stopped for diesel.

We had trouble working out the cost, with Mike trying to make himself understood.

There were, as usual, kids everywhere, and when we stopped at a bridge over a river for a break we met several kids swimming, including Manuel, aged 8, who dropped his trousers as quick as a flash and jumped in, in the nude. He was like a fish!

I took a photo of Joan removing a thorn from a little kid's foot. We gave them some bananas and they licked them and then threw the skins in the dirt. The children liked to play with my inflatable seat cushion, blowing the air out on their skin.

All along the road - the Pan American Highway, which goes down into South America - people came out of their huts to wave at us. We saw goats, pigs, great horned cows, a dead rattlesnake and a scorpion. The cows wear bells and a huge wooden block that dangles between their legs.

It was getting dark at 8pm as we followed embassy advice and turned off at Victoria for San Luis Potosí, immediately hitting mountain roads, and noticing the cooler air. With the radiator very hot, we chugged on until 11pm when we stopped in a small lay-by, noticing the road would turn sharply a few feet above us.

We watched the lights of vehicles that passed us going up and up, into the stars. Because of the heat, Mike had made a nice lemon drink in a saucepan, which he rested on the floor, and muggins promptly spoilt it by putting a foot in it! We ate a salad and Sally went for a walk up the mountain. She liked her space.

Mexico City: Streets crowded with excited fans of all nationalities, a forest of flags and banners, cars hooting, bands playing, little shoeshine boys cleaning the dust from the feet of weary travellers, riot police in buses in the shadow of side streets, the world's top soccer stars under siege in posh hotels.

That was how one radio commentator described it, but we were still hundreds of miles away!

It was Sunday June 14. We knew that England would be playing West Germany, a crucial encounter that was a replay of the 1966 final, but had no chance of listening to the match on the radio or watching it on TV. We had too much to think about, anyway; we were up at 5am, and off at 5.45. Only three of us were supposed to be up, but there were eight enjoying the wonderful views.

The roads were not for the faint-hearted; nothing between us and a sheer 1,000-foot drop. Ripper stayed by the door, open, in case he needed to leap out. Sometimes cows or donkeys were balanced on the edge. The rock was smooth, as if it has been sandpapered, and trees somehow cling to the occasional area of soil.

We drove on upwards, into the sun and the clouds, not knowing how far we would go up. The road was like a scar across the face of the mountains, which rise to 13,000 feet. Sometimes I ran behind the bus, easily keeping pace with it. That was how slow it was! Amazingly I had no trouble with asthma, which had dogged me all my life.

The bus engine was going well, but suddenly the radiator boiled over. We stopped and considered changing the thermostat to a tropical one. A lorry driver stopped. He spoke a little English and asked us what the problem was. He stayed for a while as our mechanics changed the thermostat: it took them nearly two hours.

Don drove off and we watched the reading; the temperature went up to 204 and then back to 150. It worked quite well, even though in the afternoon Roger reported the radiator indicator was always on the red. But we made it to the top.

We were almost on the Tropic of Capricorn, the sun directly overhead, hardly any shadows, and lots of flies. We refuelled at Tula on the 101, still heading for San Luis Potosi. We saw more donkeys, including four dead with buzzards flying over them, and oxen pulling carts.

My diary recorded: 'Each village, however small, has a shack advertising Coca-Cola. The village would have no electricity, but the mighty Coca-Cola company installed a fridge and a generator to keep the stuff cool. Another example of corporate values being different than the rest of us. Having said that, a cold coke in that climate I remember was very welcome. About 50 kids surrounded us at one village as we gave them some Coca-Cola we had left, and they all waved as we drove off.

'We were flagged down by a customs post for a check, and given the sad news that England had lost 3-2 to West Germany and were out of the Cup. Everyone was disappointed, but we soon got over it.'

Roger recalled: "When they lost we were gutted. But there again Bob and I (Bristol Rover supporters) unlike the rest of you were used to that feeling."

When Dave heard the news he went and shaved, washed, and cleaned his shoes. "It always makes me feel better when England lose" he said. Spoken like a true Scotsman.

We had covered 3,000 miles in 10 days and were only 140 miles from Leon, where England had been playing. It was a bitter blow, but we had lots of other things to think about, like the fact that we were almost out of food, and we had just 50 dollars left in the kitty.

There was no question that we would not carry on. Mexico City was still our destination, and we were convinced that we would earn enough money somewhere to get there, and then to carry on across Mexico and back to California, where we hoped to make quite a bit of money in the fruit fields.

We filled up with diesel at San Lui Potosi (my diary recorded: 'The city stank') and took on some water. We knew we would have to filter it because even the Mexicans wouldn't drink it. It was a slow process but it worked.

We passed dead cattle in desert conditions, yet there were tiny villages with mud, straw and wooden shacks everywhere, and chicken running about.

There were dozens of dried-up streams and riverbeds. Don estimated we were still 240 miles from Mexico City, but we remained fairly cheerful, even Ripper, who had stopped eating because of the heat, which had reached about 115F. The mountains we went through were "very small" according to the locals, but we were still very nervous as we came down next to sheer 1,000ft drops.

CHAPTER EIGHT

Now just a short diversion, lest you should think this is becoming a bit of a travelogue. I want to talk about epic journeys by bus, or by coach for that matter. The difference? I'm not quite sure; perhaps an anticipation of more comfort in the coach. We all have our own memory of long bus/coach journeys, maybe lasting a few hours up to two or three days, en route to Skeggy or a Spanish holiday resort.

I certainly remember two since I returned from my Omniworld Expo (ouch, that name still hurts) adventure – a trip to the French Alps with my wife, Nancy, when we spent about seven boring hours picking up passengers across the South of England before even reaching the Dover ferry; and a Shearings (why not name them) trip to Cornwall, when the most upbeat music the driver played the whole journey was The Old Rugged Cross and our fellow passengers were so elderly that the only time they got out of their seats was to go to the toilet or join the stampede for dinner in the hotel. We were late down one evening and they had scoffed everything except the veal, which I am not too keen on.

Others experience appalling toilet smells, pongy socks, a never-ending fear that the driver will fall asleep, travel sickness, back ache and obnoxious passengers.

I remember reading about one coach driver from Derbyshire who took a load of passengers to The Dome in London, couldn't find it and brought them all back seven hours later, and another coach party heading for the duty-free supermarkets in France, who arrived after an all-night journey to find they were closed on Sundays, and they had to go back empty-handed.

Some customers are easy to please – the elderly and slightly senile mother of one of my wife's friends went on a coach trip to Llandudno, which stopped for a break at a motorway service station, and when she and her friend didn't return on time a search party was sent out. They were discovered having coffee and cakes.

"Come on dear, we have to get to Llandudno," said a kindly friend.

"I thought this was Llandudno," said the old girl.

Many years after returning from North America I would take the bus regularly between Chesterfield and Sheffield to work and encountered many interesting passengers, including the postal worker, who said he had suffered from schizophrenia, but found religion and "the devil came out of my leg." He was now an enthusiastic born-again Christian. I was perhaps less delighted for him that I might have been, fearing that perhaps he had the devil sitting on one shoulder and a religious fanatic on the other.

And then there was the gentle spinster lady from Grassmoor, who often sat next to me and one day produced a dozen photos of herself sunbathing topless in Ibiza. "Yes, very nice," was all I could think of to say.

Anyway, let's get back to the story. I broke off from an increasingly-mundane description of our travels towards Mexico City just to say that although there were moments of drama and indeed fear in the early days of our travels, we had not yet experienced the sort of conditions that some South Americans and Himalayan passengers treat as normal, and indeed Sally and Bernice experienced later in this narrative; negotiating perilously-high and unmade mountain roads, with huge lorries and other overloaded buses heading at you at ridiculous speeds.

But, having said that, they weren't doing it in a red double-decker bus, were they!

One of the great joys about long distance travel in foreign countries is that you are never quite sure what is round the next corner. Of course, that can be one of the great disadvantages as well if you suddenly come across a bridge your bus can't get under, forcing a 40-mile detour.

We were travelling at a steady 40-50mph, which gives you plenty of time to look around and enjoy the scenery, and we could stop for photos if we wanted and if we had film in our cameras (which was in my case quite rare).

It was quite nice for those of us who were not driving or navigating to get out and stretch our legs, for, it has to be said, one could get a bit bored with the monotony of travel.

But if you think it was easy just to stop, think again! Remember, I am talking about 11 individuals, some of whom might want to stop, some who wouldn't; a casual suggestion that we stop for photos or even for the night might well, and often did, prompt a heated debate, which was likely to end with someone feeling aggrieved. Try it sometime! No, don't.

 The following day, June 15 we were off at 6.45am. We had been on the road for six weeks. We passed a dead pig with a buzzard on it and a dead dog, legs sticking up. In Britain, you didn't see dead pigs, mules or dogs by the side of the road; in Mexico they saluted you (or their legs did) every few miles.

The land was becoming more cultivated, the roads better, and there were lots of local buses. Don and Roger were working on a technique that would allow us to drive without boiling over, but as the day became warmer and the incline steeper so the radiator grew hotter.

We reached Queretaro, a cleaner town with hygienic-looking shops rather than the fly-infested meat hanging over the pavements we had seen elsewhere.

We stopped for a lunchtime break and to allow the bus to cool down, and a coach carrying the Union Jack passed in the other direction, as did several obviously English fans in cars, chanting 'England, England'. We saw a German car and a passenger leant out of the window clapping.

The road surface was good but the camber was huge, tilting the bus to a frightening degree.

By this time we were about 25 miles from Mexico City and, as we stopped to phone the British Embassy, a car pulled up and a couple from Nottingham came over. They had won a trip to the World Cup in a Shredded Wheat competition. They told us England had been a goal up against the Germans with 25 minutes left. It made the defeat even worse.

We stopped for the night at a camp site near a lake and met a car load of jolly Mexican police, like the Keystone Cops, and an English engineer, Peter, travelling with his wife and their children, who said their camper van had been attacked by German fans at Leon, ripping the English posters off. "We thought we would be safe with them, as fellow Europeans," he said.

He also said that the England team had been booed onto the pitch by Mexicans against West Germany at Leon (we lost 3-2) - the team had a reputation for being unfriendly, whilst the Germans gave out balloons and other gifts.

Mike went to a shop and found food was very cheap - three dozen oranges for four shillings (40p), bananas 6d a pound (5p), beer 1s8d (18p) and bread 1d a roll (almost free!).

My diary records: 'Roger went into the bushes and saw a snake. He froze and it went away.' We can only guess why he went into the bushes.

On Tuesday, June 16th, we drove into Mexico City and had a police escort to the British Embassy, which was just as well as we had clipped a sign and only just scraped under two bridges.

My diary recorded: 'We were met by Mr White, shortish in a suit. The bus caused a lot of interest among the women in the Embassy; they flocked out of the door and joined other women in the street, some of them leaning out of their cars whistling.

'My first impression of the city is that it is one of the most modern we have seen, biggish stores and tree-lined avenues, a really nice place that doesn't fit with the pattern of small, poor communities on the way down. It's like two countries."

It was arranged that we had a parking spot behind the Museum of Anthropology, but Pete and Sally had gone for a walk and came back with an offer to park outside an English outpost, the Piccadilly Club, run by an English girl, Jane Fernandes, and her Mexican husband, in return for free food and beer. The choice was simple. A parking lot at the Museum of Anthropology? Or Piccadilly Club and free beer? It was a no-brainer.

We got lost on the way to the club but two girls we had just met, Denise, 22, an Australian, and Maggie, 28, from London - who had come along from the Embassy for the ride - hopped out and asked some cops the way. Quite a crowd gathered while they were talking.

At the pub we had sausage and mash and a huge beer, which would have cost five pesos, but we got it free. In the evening we had roast beer and Yorkshire pud! Apparently the England team had been in the club the previous night and most of them had now flown home, which was another bitter disappointment as we had hoped to meet them.

We had picked up a packet of tea at the Embassy, which was a real pleasure, and then Roger cadged a tin of Earl Grey blend. Bob, a tea addict, was particularly pleased. English-type tea cost a packet in Mexico.

Jose, a Mexican who drove the Aussie girl, her friend and myself around the city one day, had an interesting viewpoint on the popularity of the English soccer team, or lack of it. He said everything was fine when the team arrived, but they were not allowed to mix with Mexicans, nor eat the food, and the English press had been rude about the country.

In fact, others said the same thing; one Mexican girl asked me: "Why don't English people like the Mexicans?" It seems that the press and England manager Sir Alf Ramsey had not been very diplomatic and the Mexicans were quick to take offence, particularly one channel called Channel 13.

In a letter home I wrote: 'We feel fairly safe in Mexico City, despite the fact that the English lost a lot of their support because of the unfriendly attitude of Sir Alf Ramsey.'

The streets of the city were full of peddlers selling the national lottery tickets, sweets, dolls, and statues. Many shoeshine boys sold contraceptives as a side-line, and this in a very Catholic country!

Some members of our group felt a bit lethargic because of the altitude, but not me. "You were a right one with the girls, remember that one in Mexico City with Union Jack underwear?" said Don 40-odd years later.

I thought I remembered them all, but not anyone with Union Jack underwear. Not even at half-mast! They obviously made an impression on him!

Shopping wasn't much fun without money to spend, even though it was interesting to look at the beautiful jewellery, leather clothes, bright ponchos etc. Booze was cheap – 11 pesos (7s4d old money, about 60pence today) for a half-litre bottle of Bacardi. And Roger bought a diamond ring (it was real, it cut glass) for 50 pesos (about £1.75p) after knocking the trader down from 250 pesos.

At night the city was lively, the streets lit with huge football decorations, people shouting, cars hooting. 'They all hoot like hell at the slightest hold-up, and there are always big hold-ups,' my diary recorded. 'Hooting is apparently illegal in Mexico, but they relaxed it for the World Cup. So it should be a far quieter place on our journey back to the USA.'

My diary went on: 'The people are very interested in our bus. They peer in the windows and wave and grin, very friendly. The girls look at you as you walk down the street and they don't look away, they smile and wave. I have never seen so many happy looking people. It was a delight to see the mechanics at Cummins, the big heavy transport depot, where we went on the Friday. They were always joking and smiling, and although they took a long time to get things done it proved to be a very enjoyable experience.

'We were pleased to have our lights and screens done free, but unfortunately the engine promptly developed trouble and we had to bleed the fuel injection pump several times before we corrected the trouble. For the first time we had all four flashers working together, but unfortunately the brake lights and hooter couldn't stand up to the excitement of seeing all the lights flashing, and blew up!'

We played some football against a local team, the Mexi Mechos, and then retired to the showers with them; a big room with about twenty showers and lots of little dark men with no white bathing suit marks around their thighs like we have.

Three youngsters were supposed to direct our bus back to the Piccadilly, but they got us lost, which led to trouble. There was a car behind, horn blaring, far more enthusiastic than usual, four girls and a man, hooting the English chant, waving and smiling.

We opened the back door, waved our Union Jack, blew our hunting horn, everyone was excited. They told us they could take us to the Piccadilly Club, and overtook, leading us back to the Reforma.

Suddenly the traffic lights changed to red. Look out! They stopped, and we didn't. The bus rode up on the back of their Volkswagen and fell back again. "No brakes!" shouted Dave. Everyone was silent. No-one got out of the car, but we climbed down into the rain and surveyed the damage. Luckily no-one was hurt, but the car was badly damaged.

They led us to their home. Marisella, a big-eyed Mexican girl was the driver, and she arranged for an insurance man to visit us at the club to clear repairs. Fortunately we had the same insurance company and everything was swiftly tied up. The car went into the garage next day, and we made five new friends. The brought us little gifts - a silver brooch for me and ring for David, tequilla for all. They said we must go to their party if we return this way at Christmas.

We were very impressed with the city which was modern and clean and in direct contrast to most of the country. There were people living in caves just outside the city.

On the Saturday (June 20) we were invited to play soccer against an Embassy team. Mike had arranged to take two Mexican nurses on the bus, and our group also included Alexander and Malayla from the car we hit, and several people from the embassy came too. We drove for about five miles and then held the match up, because Dave and I had to empty the toilet.

The pitch was usually dry and dusty, and the embassy staff had nicknamed it the Sahara. But this time it was really wet, and we wallowed around in the mud like hippopotamuses – got the spelling right this time! The supporters of the opposing side gave them noisy support, whilst ours were a bit quiet.

It reminds me of a pétanque match my brother, Tony, played in on the Isle of Wight, where the fans of the home pub team cheered and chanted and one subsequently said to him: "Sorry we were so loud, but we believe it helps bring out the competitive streak in them."

"We find that apathy works perfectly well," replied my brother.

Nothing would have helped us. After much panting and sliding and mud all down our legs, we lost 5-1. Or was it six? It was the first time Mike had ever played football. Malayla said she thought it was the first time I had played as well.

As for the World Cup football, Sally won two tickets to see the play-off for third and fourth place, when Germany beat Uruguay 1-0. Mike went with her. He said: 'Fantastic experience, but a fairly dull match. At least we both saw the massive Aztec stadium.

'On leaving we were being swept along by this tide of humanity, so I grabbed Sally (no easy feat) and sought the shelter of a large square pillar fearful we should get separated. When the rush subsided, we ventured out to safely and were able to find the bus directly back to Zona Rosa, where the Piccadilly Pub was.

'One of the many times the smattering of Spanish we learned in our night classes in Titusville High School, Florida, came in useful.'

Despite the fact that most of the England team had left, one day we chanced upon Geoff Hurst, Martin Peters and Peter Bonetti in a bar, but they were not that friendly or interested in us. We also met Clement Freud, the journalist and TV personality, with the stone eyes and twinkling humour, who was very funny and said he would write about us in the Financial Times.

He chatted for some time with Jan, followed her up the stairs to inspect the top deck (he was probably more interested in looking up the very short skirt she was wearing, as were the TV crew that followed them up) and then invited her out for dinner. I never did see the article.

My diary recorded: 'Roger and Bernice did well to knock down a street trader and bought a gorgeous doll for only 10 pesos. Later we heard they were being flogged for eight in the shops. Mother (Joan) was frustrated because of the lack of a launderette and is longing to have a go at washing on the stones of a river bed, as we have seen women doing on several occasions.

'I felt very safe here, unlike many of the cities in the United States, but what a perturbing place, where beggars sit in the shadow of churches filled with gold Madonnas and jewel-encrusted crosses, and a ragged woman with a thin child, so obviously homeless, sheltered for a time from the rain in a shop doorway next to the bus.'

In the evening we went to a party at Mr White's house. The bus blew hard all the way and when we arrived the house was in candlelight, not for atmosphere - because of yet another power cut across the city.

We met the genial ambassador, the tallest man in the room, wearing a white stetson and beads. The lights came on and we saw a high, white room, decorated with nets and cut out fish, coloured lights flickering and changing across the ceiling, and the most beautiful bedroom I had ever seen - a bed shaped in concrete (!), wooden panelling, soft chairs.

We arrived back at the club at about 5.30am and slept until 10am. The lads repaired the engine trouble and identified a blown fuse that had caused the lights and hooter trouble. Malayla invited us for lunch but we were too busy working on the bus.

Dave pointed out to Roger that we didn't have to leave Mexico by the 30th as we thought, as we had a permit for six months. But it had been arranged that we should go across the border at the end of the month, so we decided to leave anyway. We had watched the World Cup final on TV (we couldn't get tickets, or afford them) and Brazil had won.

As soon as it was over, we said our goodbyes and the Mexican girls cried. We drove off into heavy traffic - it was obviously a daft time to leave when the World Cup Final had just ended and everyone was on the streets, but we were caught up in the excitement.

There were Brazilian fans everywhere waving their green and yellow flags, straw boaters on the heads, singing, shouting and shaking maracas. Cars were hooting and people dancing.

We put up our Union Jack and headed down the side road and waited for our stream to merge with the rest into the chaos of a central square, the Reform.

There was no visible sign of the road, it was just a giant stage where stationary cars and buses were just props, almost submerged by waves of laughing people. We waved and hooted with the rest.

My diary recorded: 'It was such great fun, so exciting! Everyone was happy, except, perhaps, the fans of the defeated Italian team. Motorists, peering through their side windows, waved and stopped to let us through, and everywhere heads were turning. A lovely blonde, legs scorching the seams of her trousers, thrust her way through the crowds to push her hat through an open window, a German hat, blue and advertising Budweiser. 'Did you see that!' yelled Don, jubilantly flourishing it.

'Girls were everywhere, sitting on car roofs, running alongside, or noses pressed cutely against car windows. Don was out of the bus, running around the crawling cars to give his new blonde German friend a Union Jack. More people pushing round wanting to swap their hats for ours, a grin for a peace sign, blue eyes laughing into dark eyes.'

But suddenly it became scary. "Look at that lot coming," someone yelled. A huge crowd of heads, bobbing and weaving, flags fluttering, hands pointing towards us. The mood had changed; voices shouting, fewer smiles, hands thumping against the side of the bus. Our flag had been snatched by a hand from the crowd. We looked anxiously towards the dark blue police bus standing quietly in a shadow of the square, full of baton-carrying police. But they stayed where they were.

"Lock the back door, close the windows, close the curtains!" But would that increase the frenzy of hammering that shook our home? Some of the crowd had sticks. Some tried to climb in the cab, but Pete and Dave kept them out. One tried to let the air out the tyres, but Don got him out of the way. Dave drove the bus backward and forward to make it more difficult.

'Fingers scraped across the windows drawing signs - a ban the bomb sign, a peace sign, and now the 1-0 sign that insults England. We smiled through it all, me puffing my pipe.'

And gradually the crowd thinned; our Union Jack had gone, but we had a Mexican flag from a girl laughing from a car. Small children wave nervously and we wave back, relieved, glad to be out of the thick of it. Mexico City will be lively tonight but we are glad not to be there.

Soon we were out of the city and climbing again. Steep hills and the engine soon overheated. We parked up in a lay-by overnight, 30 miles from Mexico City. We had travelled 4,129 miles since we started.

CHAPTER NINE

You may wonder why we were returning to the USA instead of continuing south on our Round the World journey. The answer is simple. Money.

We had run out of funds. We knew we would find work in the USA, particularly Californian fruit fields and were confident we would avoid the need for work permits, like so many other illegals do in America.

The following morning (Monday, June 22) we drove along the Mex 15 towards Morelia and the excellent AAA elevations map indicated more hills ahead.

The bus went well, keeping just below boiling point. We passed numerous little shrines, a strange gateway in the middle of nowhere that we passed under, and a tramp with a notice that said he lived off people's generosity. The cultivated fields soon gave way to wooded mountains and S-bends every few yards, the bus climbing steadily, but balancing at a perilous angle because of the camber.

My diary recorded: 'Between Tuxpon and Puerto Garmica, at about 9,000 feet, the bus was constantly crawling along at a frightening angle. On one occasion I was sure we would not be able to make it around a bend, but we did. I ran behind the bus in the rain for a while. Mike, looking out over a sheer drop at a magnificent view, said: "To think I could never have done this before I went away!"

'There were large rocks on the road, having fallen from the slopes above. The descent was like a switchback, roads running with water, bus angling from side to side. I did not envy Dave his job at the wheel.'

At this stage I should pay tribute to the drivers and mechanics who kept us moving, Dave, Don, Roger, Bob and Pete. They were without doubt the most important members of the group, for without their mechanical skill, and the concentration and courage they displayed in driving over long distances in sometimes frightening conditions, we would have journeyed nowhere.

The towns we passed through were small and dirty. We stopped at a village where there were Indian peasants with chickens peering out of their pockets, and I also saw a pig on a lead. Mike went to get some milk, but changed his mind when he saw flies around it.

Some of the group visited a candlemaker's hut, made of mud and brick and no chimney, so smoke from the fire just found its way through holes in the roof.

"Though there was a bed and everything had its place there didn't seem to be any extras. No spare clothes or food," said Roger. An old man made candles on a machine, with five children playing around him. Next door was the village chapel, a simple building with a beautiful altar and nothing else. Not even seats.

We came upon a bridge marked four metres in height, but unfortunately we struck it, crushing the roof vents still further. There were several leaks in the roof.

We reached Morelia at about 8pm, pleased to have travelled 190 miles that day, and found a large market that was just about to close, with many vegetable stalls and a smell of fish. We had cauliflower cheese for supper. We wanted to post some mail so we headed for the airport, only to discover that it consisted of two Nissen-type huts and nothing else. So the parents will have to wait!

The following day (Tuesday, June 23) found us in flatter country and my diary recorded: 'A difficult day, less hilly but temperament (moody crew) on the bus.'

As we headed towards Guadalajara we approached rolling hills, dark blue in the distance, green, brown and red close to. We passed a brickworks, where they were baking the red clay into bricks. There were many bones along the road and we passed a dead dog with a bullet hole in the head, a dead donkey and something bigger with dogs chewing at it, possibly the carcass of a cow.

We passed 50 miles along the shores of Lago de Chapala, a lake with fishing villages, long nets drying in the sun, and then saw a street of smart street lights without any houses or proper roadway. "Someone did well to sell those lamps there," said Bernice.

Gas for our cooker cost just 40p for nearly a canister and Mike bought five punnets of strawberries for just 25p. We enjoyed them with bananas. We parked overnight near the end of the lake near a road junction. My diary recorded: 'Some fellow came to the door with his arm bleeding, having cut it to release venom after being bitten by a snake. We stopped a passing bus to take him to a doctor.'

It was very dark with rain and lightning; the only other light was from passing vehicles including buses, which occasionally stopped to let people on and off. We had a ridiculous argument about where we had bought some butter!

We started at about 8.30 am next morning and soon reached Guadalajara, stopping at a very modern shopping plaza, the best we had seen throughout the country. Enquiries led us to the address of Dr Williams, the British Consul, and we made our way along tree-lined roads to the house.

Mrs Williams, a Mexican, showed us great hospitality and treated us to some decent tea and a shower, not at the same time. Then her husband, a big, fat confident Mexican, who is medic to the Hilton Hotel, arrived. 'They have seven children and yet she is still beautiful,' my diary recorded.

They provided an interesting insight to England's World Cup fortunes; apparently when the team were staying at the Hilton before their final match, a crowd of Mexicans tried to break in, causing damage, and stayed outside all night chanting so that no-one could sleep.

Dr Williams said the team needed a better public relations man. Alf Ramsey was constantly rude to the press, and as a result they printed lies about the team not wanting to meet local people, even dignitaries. Mrs Williams observed: "If England had won the World Cup, it would have been even worse. I didn't want to be a widow!"

Mrs Williams called her cat, Lady Jane, after the wife of a former Ambassador. She told us never to open the door to people at night, which led us to a debate about what to do if someone was outside the bus trying to get in - not go out, go out in a pair, or in a group, bearing in mind that there could be 20 people outside. In those days there were no mobile phones to call the cops!

We found the people curious and friendly. We visited a market and found out that a night in a motel for two people cost just 50 pesos, which was £2, and a packet of cigarettes cost about 4p. Bob knocked down a leather waistcoat on a market stall from 120 pesos to 75 (about £2.20) but decided not to buy it.

We left the city at about 6pm and headed through more lovely scenery to a pretty little town, called Magdalena, where we stayed overnight. The church was beautiful, decorated with statues and gold and two illuminated crosses on top – 'The church seems to be where all the money is,' I observed.

Next day we started early, and it was too dark to see to the brakes which needed adjusting. Not all the vehicles use lights which can be worrying at night. Not long afterwards we came upon a crash between a coach and a car; the car driver was dead in his seat.

We saw a brightly-coloured snake dead in the road and Pete reckoned it was a deadly Coral snake. The weather was hotter with lots of flies, but Mike and I decided to run behind the bus as it slowly progressed up a mountain road. Mike dropped out, but I carried on and on, and in a coach behind passengers appeared to be timing me, which made me feel like a marathon runner!

We stopped at the River Santiago for a refreshing swim. Lorries were loading sand and pebbles. One driver had a muzzle-loading gun; we speculated he had it for snakes, of which we saw many. Roger and Bob repaired an oil leak on the rear brake and adjusted the others. We drove 200 miles in the day.

On Friday, June 26 we reached the Pacific at Mazetlan, marvelling at how blue it was, but we didn't have much time for sightseeing - our first priority was to find some chemicals for the toilet (at a chemist) and the next to do something about a large stone lodged in the rear nearside wheel. But none of the jacks worked

It was very hot. We stopped for lunch at a monument which marked the Tropic of Cancer. We were passing through very dry country, mostly light brown scrubland and hardly any green trees.

A petrol tanker pulled up and dropped off an Englishman called Clive Holloway, in his early 20s, red hair, very tanned, who was hitching his way around the world, fishing everywhere he went, sponsored by two fishing tackle firms. He said he had caught a sailfish off Mazatlan the day before. We gave him a ride as far as Culcacan.

We passed through a noisy electrical storm, fork lightning crackling all around us like exploding fireworks. Very impressive. The road was very bad because we had to use diversions because of road works. We stopped for the night after 200 miles and the night shift discovered we had run out of water, yet we had only filled the tank the day before. It was a very warm - and thirsty - night.

As we moved on, we travelled into an area where efforts at irrigation were being made, canals, ditches and scrub clearance. We saw a dead horse, still half upright, tied to a post.

It was very hot and as soon as we found a tap to fill up the water tank we did so, and enjoyed lemon drinks. We drove for six hours without seeing a town, then passed Navoaja and finally Guyames, a wealthy-looking place, despite a shanty town area down the hillside.

We continued on Mex 15 across a low flat plain that was almost a desert. In places the land is being reclaimed and was well irrigated making a pleasant change to the scenery.

Not far from Guaymas we were stopped by a car carrying Clive, our hitch-hiker friend from yesterday. They told us of a good beach to park up at overnight. We arrived in the area of the Mazatlan beach and were then stopped by another car containing two people.

One, Joan Billington, came from London and could hardly believe her eyes at seeing a red double-decker bus. They guided us to the beach, which is owned by Paramount film studio and was used as the location set for the film 'Catch 22.'

Within minutes of our arrival we were all in swimming costumes and diving into the Pacific Ocean. The water was very warm and clear. Later we made a cup of tea and Joan expressed the view that she never thought she would be drinking Earl Grey tea in a double-decker bus by the beach.

Joan invited us to her house for a shower and she and her fiancé, Alvin P Rothschild, took us out to dinner. We returned to the beach and got a campfire burning, and enjoyed a few beers provided by some young Americans. There was a unanimous decision to stay for a few hours tomorrow and enjoy a rest.

It was Saturday 27 June 1970. We had travelled 350 miles that day and felt we deserved a rest. Our total distance covered since Montreal was 5,264 miles.

Many of us were up early next day and went swimming. It was a very hot day, but there was a nice breeze from the sea. In the afternoon one of the American girls from the beach party, Lisa Irion, came down and invited us to go water skiing.

Mike and Dave went along. Dave remembers: "We had a ball. I managed to get up and stay up for a little distance, but Mike tended to get up and then sit down again. Still we had a good time."

Most of us had a nice a tan, in Bernice's case very red, with swollen eyes!. In the evening we left the beach and drove through the cool of the night. We passed through Hermosillo and onto Santa Anna. With Dave on first shift at the wheel we drove non-stop for 24 hours towards the border with the USA, across a desert, in dust storms, very hot, 180 miles without passing a building.

We stopped on a dry salt lake to buy huge quantities of melons and other fruit (which we thought we had to eat before we reached the USA) and salad, over a range of mountains with terrifying drops, and finally to the border at about 6am.

There were long queues of traffic at Tijuana waiting to cross. The Customs people looked us over carefully and had a chat and told us we could have brought in the melons without them being confiscated. My poor stomach!

They were very friendly and showed us around. One man sits in a window behind a Venetian blind using binoculars to look over the cars and occupants, hoping to spot anyone looking nervous who might be bringing in drugs or illegal immigrants. They kept in touch with the checkpoint by walkie-talkie.

We were through by 9.30am and stopped at a garage to clear out and recharge our water tanks. It was much cooler and there was a huge difference in our surroundings; cultivated fields where there had been barren desert, concrete buildings where there had been wooden shacks.

We headed off along the main road towards Los Angeles, stopping outside a bank at a place called Cardiff on the Beach. An Englishman turned up, amazed to see us, and in conversation I discovered his name was Peter Scott Jackson and he was the brother of my old French teacher in the Isle of Wight! What a small world!

CHAPTER TEN

We had just 27 dollars in the kitty, so we were in desperate need of some fund-raising ideas to make sure we could continue to eat, as well as to put diesel in the tank! Did we panic? You bet we did!

We were told that that there was a horse fair a few miles back, where we might be able to sell our horse brasses, but when we arrived the organisers said it was not possible. But something always turns up (well, nearly always) and before we finally committed ourselves to putting the girls on the streets (just a joke) fate intervened on our side.

Back on the road and into San Diego we stopped at a British-style pub, Scotties, and they directed us to Boom Trenchard's Flare Path, next to the airport, where there was already a Bristol 1952 double-decker, which had been entered in a double-decker bus race the following weekend. Apparently there were several double-decker buses in the area, linked to pubs and restaurants.

Another coincidence, and this time we might make some money from it, and publicity. The Boom is under the flightpath so very noisy and we decided to move on next to a lake, and were then moved on again by police, who said trailer parks were the only option. We headed out of the city to find somewhere free to stop overnight.

Next day (a Wednesday) we drove back to the Boom and the owner, Larry Calder, said he would sponsor us in the race for $100 and a meal a day. Food and fuel! We decided to stay until Sunday.

San Diego was a beautiful city, comfortably warm, nice beaches, huge surf, lots of parks and modern architecture. I contacted the local radio station and newspaper, Joan did the washing, and Pete made $130 selling brasses. Rog, Bernice and I did a recording on Channel 8 TV and watched a nice long piece that was broadcast in the evening.

'We have had a couple of free meals and our finances have improved, recovering from 18 dollars to over $300 in two days!' my diary recorded.

A lad called Fred arranged for us to park up at a parachute school run by an English lady, Marjorie Forrest, from Manchester. She was delighted to meet us and see the bus. She invited us to have some training and to do a parachute jump. Pete and Dave said yes, but the rest were a bit dubious.

After the weeks of travel and lack of a social life in Mexico, life improved considerably, including a visit to Sea World on Thursday 2 July 1970. The local TV company came with us and made a film. They said I did a good interview. We watched it later when we went back to Boom Trenchards for a meal and some beer. The place was leaping and great fun.

A note here about drinking. I like a pint. So did all the blokes on the bus. Usually, we didn't have the money to have any beer, but occasionally, when the bus was parked up for a promotion, we had free beers and often our very generous American/Canadian friends treated us.

American beer is not as nice as British or Belgium beer. The cruel critic could say it lacks taste and bite. But it is stronger than you think, particularly if you have had several and if the weather is hot.

I have had some drunken moments. As a young man I remember throwing up in the toilets at the Beachcomber Bar in Shanklin, and noticing a familiar octave in the throat of the person throwing up in the neighbouring loo, I enquired if it was my brother and it was.

That was my older brother. My younger brother once (on the occasion of his stag night) lashed himself (mentally) to the throne in my older brother's home and we could NOT prise his hands free. We left him moaning there for several hours.

The most drunken man I ever saw (on his feet) was attempting to cross a bus station in Finland, three steps forward, two sideways and one backward. He made it after 15 minutes. For those with a long memory, the late comic Jimmy Wheeler would have been impressed as the drunk he created in his act was remarkably similar.

My own most drunken moment must have been in middle-age, at a travel company reception for journalists – I believe the hosts were Busch Gardens – in Manchester when the red wine flowed freely and I was the last to rise from the long dinner table and headed for the exit. I made my way past the empty chairs along the wall, and as I neared the end towards the door there was an old tired-looking chap coming along the wall towards me, and politely I gestured with my hand for him to turn through the door first. He didn't say anything, but gestured at me. "No, after you," I insisted, but the silly sod remained rooted to the spot, still gesturing… and I realised I was looking in a mirror! From such moments, sobriety is born.

Back in San Diego, we chatted up some girls at Boom Trenchards and I drove one of them to her home in a VW Beetle. It was crazy, the first time I had driven in the USA, and I was only a little more sober than she was. I nearly drove up the exit of the Freeway! Next morning she had gone to work when I woke and I somehow found a local bus that took me back to the harbour and my fellow travellers.

It was Independence Day, July 4th, and we headed for the San Diego Stadium for the bus race. There were four buses, one from LA, and it was obvious from the start that they were lighter and faster than us; we had a water tank, bunks, a toilet and a kitchen weighing us down. It was a Le Mans type start, the great 24-minute bus race, watched by a few hundred people.

Roger was first upstairs to touch the window and first away, but within half a lap all the others had passed us. Booms' bus was by far the fastest and did 12 laps compared to our nine. Which was not too bad. Anyway, we made money from it!

Afterwards we went back to Booms, then to Mission Beach, and Mike and I went off with another girl we had met, Chris, to a beach party. Dave and Pete went parachuting and couldn't find us later.

San Diego School of Sport Parachuting, Inc.
LAKESIDE, CALIFORNIA

Know all ye men that on the **4** day of **July**

in the 19**10**th year of our Lord; Being of sound mind and body

David T. McLaughlin

did alone and unassisted depart from an aircraft at an altitude of 3000 feet and safely navigate to the ground by parachute.

Dennis Sattler   **CESSNA 185**
D-2542
INSTRUCTOR   AIRCRAFT

Dave's diary records: 'Without doubt it is one of the most wonderful things I have experienced. The peace and solitude as one floats down has to be experienced to be believed. The inner feeling of contentment and achievement is absolutely tremendous – and all within the three minutes before you land.'

We left San Diego the following day for Los Angeles, passing through places we had heard the names of on TV or in films, Long Beach, Newport Beach, Ocean Beach, and then Watts, where there was a huge black population. Mike shopped at a store and was the only white customer.

Cautiously we crept under a bridge marked 13ft 9ins, and eventually found our way to Marina del Ray, where we parked overnight and were given permission by the Marina City authorities to stay for a few days AND use their toilets and shower, a luxury!

It was a boating marina being built on marshland, complete with apartments. Roger and Bernice left for a few days to stay with relatives and I was in charge. I arranged to ring them every morning at 9.30 am, and got on with telephoning local newspapers and TV and radio stations in the hope of getting publicity and maybe some promotion work.

One TV station came round to do an interview with me and the cameraman followed Jan up the stairs and showed her bottom under the short skirt. My interview didn't stimulate half as much interest.

A local resident, Betty, and her daughter, Janine, 16, took us to the shops in their car, and told us about two bars/restaurants, the Mucky Duck and the Tudor House, where we managed to sell $80 of horse brasses! They own a catamaran, the Kata Maru, built in their back garden over five years, which they plan to sail to Hawaii as soon as Betty's husband learns his navigation. It was cool here, 70 or 80 F compared to 110 a few miles inland, and, apparently, mountain skiing six hours north!

Don and I visited the British Consul, General Bernard Bull, and his staff, who had gone to great trouble to find us addresses where we could sell our brasses and other British goods. But generally it is difficult to find ways of making money.

After looking through newspaper ads, Sal, Joan, Bob and Don looked like they had found work around the boatyards, but Roger pointed out there were possible complications for us if we had to get social security numbers while on our visitor visas, so they gave it up.

In Britain, as I wrote this in 2014, immigration and illegal workers were, as now, a controversial topic, largely because successive Governments failed to control it and because the recession resulted in a huge rise in unemployment. People resent what they see as foreigners coming in and taking their jobs.

In those days in the USA there was a huge influx of illegal immigrants working across the fruit fields, and often the authorities turned a blind eye to it because they worked for low wages and the fruit farmers made big profits, which in turn helped the local and state economy. Business is so closely allied to politics in the US that if you know the right people you can avoid minor inconveniences like visits from immigration officials.

Unlike your normal 'wetback' – the term used to describe Mexicans, who entered Texas by crossing the Rio Grande river – we had no intention of staying in the US permanently.

We needed to work to get money to continue our journey, but we had to be careful about working without permits and attracting attention, and we certainly could not go down the road of providing the authorities with false information in order to get social security numbers.

Los Angeles was a smoggy, sprawling city of several districts each with their own shopping centre, and difficult to get around without a car. It was impractical to drive the bus everywhere.

But we needed to travel to find work options. Roger tried for several days to get a free car from BOAC and other sponsors, but failed, and eventually we had to pay out $11.50 a day. We had a few rows on the bus about that! That's what happens when money is short.

In a letter home I said: 'The States is in a bad financial state right now and we haven't made money as quickly as we hoped. But we do get free fish and chips (from the Royal London fish bar, run by Bill Kelly from Blackpool and his family. All English food, a pint of Watney's Red Barrel, and even the cod is from Grimsby)!

'I'm sure it will be better soon because we hope to get some cash from fruit picking. It was good to get letters from home. I had 26 today! One of us didn't get any, but he hadn't written home at all.'

Not sure who that was, Pete maybe?

Two girls, who we had met earlier in Mexico, left a message with a mailman that they were looking for us, and Dave and I found them at a nearby supermarket. We went to an English pub, Ye Mucky Duck, in the evening. It was one of the most authentic pubs we had yet seen, with two dart boards. Pete managed to sell $39 worth of horse brasses and was really pleased.

The girls came back to the bus to say hello; however, they didn't stay long. I sensed some hostility.

I was resting on my bunk (the only privacy we had) with one of them, Denise, as the bus journeyed along the road, discussing the attractions of Australia, when Bernice came up, reached through the curtains and said: "We're sharing out the Coca-Cola and this is your share.'

An awkward moment. We got the message. The girls left.

Our hosts at Marina City suggested we leave because although they had gained some publicity through us, they were annoyed at having to receive some phone calls. Bob had an upset stomach for about a week (too much fish and chips?) but Sal cured it with some medicine. Healing hands.

We were visited by Cyril Maitland, who was a freelance photographer for the English national newspapers. Interest in the bus had increased following the article in the LA Times and more people were aware of us as we drove around.

As a result of our visiting Ye Mucky Duck pub we made contact with some people who lived in a commune just up the road. They invited us to move the bus onto a piece of their land and we could stay as long as we like. There were seven adults and a couple of children on a nice spot close to the Santa Monica beach.

We were staying at 314 Margarita Avenue, an old house with a large garden, fountains and a tree house. I wrote home: 'I am sitting in the garden of a house where we have parked our bus. There are 28 cats! The seven adults all live together and share bills and eat together, and they are all professional people in their 20s, a lawyer, banker, teacher etc. My asthma has come back, and I'm not sure if is the cats or the polluted air. We shall stay here for a month or more.'

Joan also developed an allergy.

We were made very welcome by the couple in charge, Elliott E Welch II and his wife, Peggy, who have the children. They had a gripe box, not a bad idea for a group of people who might fall out over little unspoken differences. Maybe we should have had one.

"We are not really a commune, more a co-operative" Elliott explained. He was tall and bespectacled, bearded with receding hairline. Their lounging room was covered with mattresses, and there was a blank wall where people could write.

They handed me a pencil. "Write anything" they said, but my mind went blank. Later I wrote a poem. Not a very good poem. We ate corn on the cob, which they had grown, and listened to recordings of the Goon Show, of which Elliott had 20. And we blocked the toilets; four out of six out of action after the first day!

Elliott had gained national fame (or infamy) for his fight against a three-year prison sentence for refusing to be conscripted. He gave notice of a conscientious objection, but said his objection was not a religious one, but a moral one. It took a five-year battle before the Supreme Court quashed his sentence. He said he would have fled to Canada if he had lost.

My diary reads: 'Elliott is very pessimistic about the future. Pollution or collapse of the system will, he feels, bring about either mob rule or the military will take control. California, for example, depends completely on water being pumped in from Toronto miles away, air conditioning and irrigation, and if that failed no-one would be able to survive.'

He also smoked a lot of marijuana. Everyone did.

Another resident was Trevas, who was getting married to his partner the following week. He was a teacher on the history of film. He aimed to make a film every two years and at that moment was working on a film about a 'free school', where kids, aged five to 14, could come and go as they pleased and do exactly what they wanted.

He said it enabled the children to discover exactly what they were good at, maths, maybe, or fishing, or woodwork, and concentrate on that. Sounds idealistic, but hardly a rounded education! At the time, I was persuaded it was not just a good but brilliant idea. Strange what funny fags do to you.

On the bus there was a general discussion about wages; if we managed to get jobs, should the money go to the bus or to the individual?

That led to a debate about the British welfare and social security system, with Roger and Dave arguing one way and Joan and Don another. I don't think we reached a conclusion about wages, so the existing system stood – the bus got the money!

As in any relationship, money, who spends it and how it is spent, was a big issue. It is an interesting thought that although we were being hosted by a self-styled co-operative, in fact, we on the bus were probably more of one than they were. We pooled all our money and all our energies, to the extent that as individuals we had virtually no money to spend on ourselves. Which made life particularly difficult when we were settled in one spot.

On the road we were united in the purpose of raising enough money to continue the trip. When we stopped, we were subject to the usual temptations, mostly shopping and going out for an evening's entertainment, usually in a bar.

Often, we were lucky enough to be invited out and didn't need to spend much, but that sometimes seemed like sponging. And as the singles usually had more invitations than the couples, it could also cause tensions. We were a squabbling family, fused together by need but likely to split into factions or even individuals at any time.

However, our first priority as a group was to find paying work!

Our first avenue of endeavour was usually sponsorship, because it generated more money than individual effort, and meant less work; we either carried an advertisement for the sponsor on the side of the bus, or parked outside their restaurant or bar to attract customers. It was not straight-forward; we thought we had lined up Schweppes for a deal, they had their adverts printed and ready to go, and then their budget was clipped. BOAC also had their budget cut.

The British Consul were continuing to be extremely helpful despite the fact that a previous group, who visited LA travelling in a single-decker bus (how boring), became an embarrassment, leaving a trail of debt. On three occasions they pretended that their bus had been stolen, just for publicity.

We discovered that a red double-decker was no longer much of a novelty in LA, as several restaurants had one and you could hire them for 60 dollars a day from a Long Beach firm. But gradually we found opportunities.

John McInnes, a former Coldstream Guard who sold British goods in his uniform, had introduced us to the Royal London Fish and Chip Shop and we flogged brasses, flags and maps to visitors, and then shopkeepers invited us to do the same; we were making about 10 dollars a day, enough for food.

Back to the social events: Commune residents Lynette and Trevas got married in the garden. Danny, the gardener, was also a minister, and performed the ceremony. The couple had written their own ceremony taking many of the words from American Indian ceremonials and from Buddha. Dave said it was a very sincere ceremony, which seemed to contain much more meaning than many church ceremonies.

The wedding took place in a flower-adorned gazebo in the garden. The bride wore flowers and a flowing gown, brown, I think. I wore a dinner jacket and black bow tie without a shirt, and brown hot pants.

There were lots of poems and sentimental ballads. I smoked an animal skin-covered pipe (later, back home in England, our dog Smithy used to curl his lip and show his teeth at it) containing a mixture of blackcurrant-flavoured tobacco and marijuana, and I was still puffing on it when I was introduced to a judge. I enjoyed it all very much.

As a matter of interest, I had only tried pot for the first time a few weeks earlier whilst listening to a recording of the newly-released Jesus Christ Superstar. It was relaxing, and concentrated the mind somewhat, and I remember being spellbound by the music. I enjoyed it while I was in California and Florida, but never smoked it again after I left. Of course, I didn't inhale.

Our fund-raising efforts continued. It was Thursday 16 July 1970. One of the products we had been promoting came from a UK company called Control Packaging and was a new way to fasten products. Following earlier contact, a Mr Price Barion came to see us and said he would like to manufacture it in the US under licence. A cable had been sent to the company about this, but they said they would not allow their product to be manufactured under licence. A full explanation was on its way, but it was a disappointment. This happened several times; we lined up a good order and then the UK manufacturer could, or would not, meet it.

We had a three-day promotion at a fish and chip bar in Culver City. It was run by Millie and Fritz Nielson. She was English and he Danish.

We parked outside the shop and business was quite brisk with a steady stream of shoppers. The bus was open to view and we sold $42 worth of horse brasses as well as some products from Buckingham Palace Imports. We also had two free meals. Back at the house we were taken to a pop concert by Suzie and Peggy.

Don and Bob had got a job painting a doctor's surgery, so they did not come with us to Culver City for our second day. This was again quite successful and we sold £93 worth of kit. Sally, Bernice and Roger went baby-sitting in the evening."

I was hitching a lift to San Diego to see Chris, a very hot day but no trouble getting lifts. One young fellow picked me up at Oceanside; he was very enthusiastic about a new product called Sta-Power. Under the dark glasses was Bruce Kats, a former marine PE instructor, discharged because of a leg injury, who agreed to meet Rog and I at a bar near Disneyland the next week.

As a result we tested Sta-Power, which was a diesel additive, designed to give extra mileage, and despite inconclusive conclusions (there was no apparent benefit to our fuel consumption), we attended a Sta-Power conference intending to praise the product to all corners of the earth if we were paid handsomely to do so!

The Sta-Power President walked through a mass of near-hysterical delegates, all intent of being noticed or perhaps even to touch the Great Man, and from the stage he congratulated a long list of delegates, who had made the most money selling the stuff. From the frenzy surrounding him we wondered if it was a pyramid scheme, where members get paid for enrolling as many other members as possible and one day it would all come crashing down: "He didn't write the Bible, he only corrected it," observed one man, hoping, like the rest, to make millions. The brand still exists today, however, so we must have been wrong.

We were making money for the bus, but not much for ourselves.

In a letter home to her grandmother and aunt, Sal wrote: 'Haven't been able to buy anything. Had $7 pocket money in three months, and that's gone on letters, postcards and stamps.

'Guess what I'm doing with the nighties you made me? One I've shortened and wear over my trousers, looks great. The other I have taken in and wear it as a dress! Very fashionable around California.'

She added that she didn't like the way children in California were brought up with 'this lark of free expression, in other words no discipline at all and very spoilt.'

Sally said that lots of young people were rebelling against going to Vietnam, and also observed: 'American men are more polite and better behaved towards women. Clothes are brighter, cheaper, and much less conventional. I love American steaks and hamburgers. I would not live here for long, though!'

In a letter home, dated August 2nd or 3rd, I wrote: 'We are making more cash now as we get some work. We have been renovating a mobile home for 250 dollars, about £105. Only trouble is that one of us drove it into a telegraph pole and smashed the back, which was expensive. When I get some cash I will start repaying my debts. We had a good chance of making a lot of money when a big businessman over here said he would sell our packaging catch on licence in the States, but the English manufacturers said they were not ready to export! Maybe that's why we are not the power we were.

'On Monday we met a Senator Roberts, a friend of Barry Goldwater (former Presidential candidate). Roberts was drunk and became embroiled in a stupid argument about Vietnam with two American girls, Chris and Mollie, and me, and made a complete fool of himself. It's a bit worrying to think that he has a lot of power.

'On the bus we continue to have a lot of arguments and usually the crew are split into two parts. It is a sad state of affairs really. There was a big row yesterday when two were threatened with being thrown off, and since then the air has cleared a bit.'

Perhaps we stayed too long. Pete, who had been trying to come to terms with the breakdown of his relationship since nearly the start of the trip, suddenly announced he was leaving. It was a blow but he was determined and it was probably the right decision.

Dave recorded: 'Pete has decided to leave the bus. This has been brewing for some time and he has been searching around in LA for jobs. When we got up his bags were packed and off the bus. We all said goodbye to him and wished him luck. This is the first departure of a crew member and is a disappointment even if half expected. He is going to stay at the house for a while until he is organised.'

The remaining ten of us were ready to get back on the road.

The bus needed fixing. As Dave's diary recorded: 'Our oil seal problem has continued to be a concern, so today we went to a garage to get it fixed. When the rear differential was drained large chunks of metal also came out and this caused some consternation. It is possible that the bearing is cracking up or even the bearing housing. As there was no heavy lifting equipment about we could not do the job anyway, so it was decided to leave it for a few weeks and keep an eye on it. The oil seal was changed and the brakes adjusted. Some maintenance still needs to be finished but we will do it on Wednesday.'

As previously mentioned, I had little to offer in the way of assistance to the mechanics apart from muscle if heavy bits needed to be lifted. Usually I busied myself with my diary or contacting the local media. Some played Monopoly. I learnt to hate the game.

We had not realised that the waste water from the sink had gathered under the bus.

With the bus repaired, we tried to drive off, to attend a party. It sank into the soft ground and we had to dig the wheels out.

With Don supervising operations, we jacked the wheels up. Jan, by mistake, fell through the hatch in the floor and ended up covered in evil-smelling mud.

Dave was helping Mike do some cine film for his children, in the garden and on the cliff top. Returning to find Don and Bob jacking the wheels up, Dave suggested they needed to get a tow out of the mud, as we will not do it any other way. When his idea was roundly rejected Mike and Dave went to the beach and finished off their filming.

When they returned, the bus was still bogged down and there had been no improvement despite hours of work. A young lad was there who had a van. Dave asked him to hook up on the front and give the bus a little forward tension, so he could drive it out. He agreed and the bus was out. One brownie point for Dave.

My impressions of Los Angeles? 'Sprawling, hot, smog that sneaks up on you making the eyes water, tall white buildings, fast freeways, a nine-storey road junction complex.

'Santa Monica is said to have more British residents than any other US city, but we haven't seen many of them.

'The Mucky Duck is probably the most realistic British pub we have seen, leaning on the bar, Watneys at 25p for a half pint. Santa Monica beautiful, Venice scruffy, Beverley hills elegant, Watts foreboding, San Fernando Valley an oven.'

In a letter home I added that it was such a big city that you felt quite detached from Hollywood, the film stars and the Manson trial, although the newspapers were full of it. 'Today I spoke to a girl who went to school with Judy Garland's younger daughter. The young people we meet here are pretty way out, often long-haired druggies. It's a weird, bored community, lots or murders. Seven policemen are on manslaughter charges for accidentally shooting to death two Mexicans who hadn't done anything.'

A letter home like that would have done a lot to reassure my mother!

CHAPTER 11

What do US politicians and British MPS have some common? Not a lot. OK, they are both elected. But in the US, a senator or congressman has considerably more power, not just by voting, but by influence.

We found that out to our advantage after the police ordered the bus off the road for being too high. It was something we had expected to happen since we landed in Montreal four months before, but the reality was a devastating blow.

We sat around our Santa Monica base, gazing through dust-streaked windows at posh homes and palm trees, and wondered if red tape would put us off the road for good, where natural obstacles had failed.

Wednesday 22 July 1970 had certainly proved to be an interesting day as officialdom reared its ugly head. We left Canoga Park planning to complete our maintenance checks at a garage and as we travelled along the San Diego Freeway we noticed a Highway Patrol police car had pulled in behind us and was just tagging along.

As we left the Freeway the HP police car was still with us and flagged us down. They then escorted us to a car park where the officers told us that an official in the State department of Highways had made a complaint that we were an over-height vehicle travelling without a permit.

This had been about two weeks ago, but no action had been taken. On Tuesday a further complaint had been made and so the police had to act.

Fortunately they did not book us for any offence, Roger's IPA membership again came in very useful, but they did escort us back to the house and told us we were grounded until we had sorted out permits.

We talked with some LAPD officers later about what had happened. They were furious that the HP police had come onto city streets and stopped us. It is not their jurisdiction apparently. We contacted the Department of Highways but they were not helpful. They said they would give us a permit to get out of the state but that was all. Roger phoned the consulate to see if they can help.

In a letter home, I said: 'We were stopped by police yesterday because we were ten inches too high for their roads, and told this morning that the only place we could move was out of California! Not even 100 yards to a store!'

Potentially, it could have ended our trip. We were banking on an extended stay in California to earn money by working in the fruit fields.

Without that money we wouldn't be able to afford to go very much further. And if the Californian authorities had stopped us, then no doubt the police in neighbouring states would be alerted, and do the same thing. But we weren't about to give in that easy.

Roger and I telephoned all the LA TV and radio stations and the newspapers, and our local contacts, and soon our plight was hitting the airwaves. 'Bus adventure falls foul of red tape' and 'Cops take Brits off road' screamed the headlines. One newspaper had a photograph of me on a child's trike in front of the bus, and queried: "Which will he drive?"

EVENING OUTLOOK   Friday, July 24, 1970—17

Which Will He Drive?

Britisher John Winter tries a tricycle after learning that the double - decker bus which he and 10 other Englishmen hope to drive around the world is too high to drive on state highways. State Sen. Robert Stevens is trying to get the group a special permit to use their bus. (Evening O...

Our plight captured the imagination of the always friendly and courteous Californians, but it also excited the interest of a very senior resident, State Senator Robert Stephens, who, perhaps seeing some political capital in it, took action to speed us on our way.

'We have the OK to go anywhere, almost, from Senator Stephens,' I wrote home. 'He put pressure on the highways department. His secretary told them: "Are you going to give them a permit, or is your successor?"'

Dave's diary captured the crisis as follows: 'Thursday 23 July 1970 - John telephoned The Times and Evening Outlook and explained what had happened. They are interested in a story. The Outlook phoned the state capitol to see what could be done and was told 'Nothing' which did not impress them.

'A local radio station became involved and when they phoned Sacramento they were told there was no problem. Roger phoned the Highways Department and spoke to a Mr Bobo. He was very unhelpful and rather rude. He flatly refused to give us any permit except to get out of the state.

'By now matters were really warming up. A phone call brought in a previous contact, Alvin Rothschild, and he put us in touch with a Representatives office that referred us to the mayor's office and then an Assemblyman. We got two Vehicle Code references, 35780 and 35719, under which we should be able to get a permit. Mr Bobo still refused to issue a permit.

'We then tried the Governor's office who told us to contact a State Senator. We did this and got to the office of Senator Robert Stephens. His secretary, Phyllis Taylor, listened to our problem and was on our side. She discussed the matter with the senator who told her to get us the permits. She phoned Mr Bobo and who again refused to issue permits and was rude to her.

'She advised the senator of her lack of progress and then phoned Mr Bobo again. This time she got the permits.

'She felt that her remark "Would you like to issue the permits or would you rather your successor did" may have done the trick.

'Whilst all this was going on The Outlook did a story. A female reporter came down to interview the girls for their story and a story was passed by phone to Today reporter Tom Riney. He wrote an article blasting officialdom, but once he found out that Senator Stephens had resolved the issue he had to change it. Phyllis Taylor came to visit us and told us about events of the day and that should there be any further problems all we had to do was contact her.'

We got the permit. And a commitment from the police Highway Patrol to help us in any way they could as we continued through the state. How about that!

But there were other problems. Our long stay in California, and the warm welcome we received from the people we met, combined to present us with a problem; the fact that some of us (the unattached ones) were often invited out on our own, sometimes overnight, and sometimes into relationships that lasted more than the odd night.

In my case I found the American girls very friendly and accommodating, so much so that I was often on the fringe of a party lifestyle that distracted me from the bus.

It was a chance to chat intimately with someone outside the usual group, and thus share problems and confidences; and most of all have some fun, which was not always the case within the rigid regime we had adopted to survive so far. It led to tensions with the 'married' couples.

Anyway, back to the diary. We had borrowed a car from a new friend, Jack, just to get to the shops, etc.

Now the bus had its permit, Dave and Bob tried to return it to the garage but no-one was there so they drove back.

We were also delayed in leaving the city because Don had a bad eye infection and needed to see a specialist about it. It was diagnosed as a cyst, caused by dust in the eye, and cut out with the help of four injections and eye clamps. Don came back from the Santa Monica Medical Centre 28 dollars worse off, but that was after a 15-dollar discount.

We spent some time being photographed by Mark Douglas for Woman's Weekly, and then went and relaxed on the beach or in the crashing surf.

The car was returned, and we left Los Angeles about 8pm. There was one nasty moment when Dave crawled to a halt in the second lane of a busy freeway, while we checked the height of an overpass with car lights hurtling past on both sides, but the bus scraped under. We spent the night in a garage just before the mountains.

It was Wednesday, August 12, as we drove up into the mountains on Route 5, and very hot in the valley, about 110F.

We stopped to adjust the engine – "to get air out of the whatsits" was my very technical diagnosis.

We travelled 200 miles to Fresno, the middle of the grape-growing industry, and obtained a permit to go to King's Canyon the following day.

At a loose end, we were invited to a tennis club for a swim by a local resident, Bob Bogesian, the civil servant who had issued us our permit. He phoned his wife, who was quite bemused to hear she had to do an immediate shop for a BBQ with 10 English people on a DD Bus. However she rose to the occasion and we had a great evening.

Ripper asked Mrs Bog, a mother of four: "Is there much breeding going on around here?"

She was taken aback for a moment, and then said: "You mean cattle?"

He did. She said there was some.

She liked Governor Reagan, which was unusual amongst people we had talked to.

It was so hot that several of us slept outside the bus on the grass. King's Canyon was beautiful. I had toothache and spent much of the day on Panadol. To get there we had had to drive amongst mountains that reached up to 6,500 feet, poor winding roads, great views, but the driver had to concentrate.

I wrote home: 'The road we are going up now is very narrow in places – it twists and turns up to 6,000 feet and sometimes there is only about two feet of road between us and a terrible drop! We take it very carefully and Mike is usually standing at the back ready to jump out. He hates heights, and in fact he must be the world's worst traveller because he can't stand planes, ships or roads. I don't know why he came he hates travel so much, but he is very brave to keep going,'

We reached the settlement of Grant's Village, and in a temperature of 100F walked (or in the case of Sal, Dave and I, ran) to the Giant Tree, a 260-foot tall-redwood, 3,000 to 3,500 years old, 107.6 feet in circumference, amongst other huge trees that had great burns from lightning strikes, forest fire and Indians. One fallen tree was known as the Fallen Monarch, and people had lived inside it.

Then we drove down to beautiful Lake Hume, a base for up to 800 Young Christians each week, where we had a cool swim. My diary recorded 'meditated for 50 minutes' before we ate hot dogs. I can't believe that. Not if we were hungry. Not in any circumstances. Well, perhaps if money was involved.

The scenery we encountered was the most spectacular we had seen, but the drawback was I had no film for my camera with which to record it. 'I have been down to two cents for a week, and had to borrow to get some toothpaste,' I noted. 'It's a bit off when everyone else, except Sal, buys souvenirs and drinks.'

I had a further reflective moment on my own position. My diary recorded: 'All these wonderful views, it would be nice to share them with someone else, as it would each other experience, the ordeals, parties, joys and hardships. How strange to share a trip with nine other people and yet be lonely.'

As you will recall, most of us were in our 20s and subjected to the usual fancies that 20-somethings suffer, i.e. birds or blokes and booze. I was obviously missing the female company we had enjoyed in San Diego and Los Angeles, particularly Chris, who had stayed with us for a few days before we moved on. Everyone loved Chris. It was sad to lose contact with her.

Anyway, back to earth in King's Canyon; there was smoke over the trees and it turned out to have been a forest fire, the third in three days, which destroyed two acres before 30 men managed to control it. In the winter, we were told, there was up to 10 feet of snow there.

Locals told us that they had to shoot a bear because it caused a nuisance to visitors. They came in for food after their hibernation, and trashed the place.

Nonetheless, we decided to sleep out again, because it was so hot. I woke up half way through the night and spotted a bulky, dark creature at the edge of the trees and decided to move into the bus for safety.

Next morning, I said: "Did you see that bear last night?"

"Which bear?"

"It was roaming around the campsite. You must all have been asleep. I went into the bus and slept there."

"What, and left us outside with a bear?"

They were quite indignant. I can't see why.

We ate breakfast of flapjacks and sausage meat, and loads of coffee, with the camp owner, and then drove back towards Fresno, stopping at Reeding, where we had arranged to get some free fruit from a Mr Peters, who turned out to be a Bible-basher and the local police chief.

We were guided to a place by the river, Lindy's Landing, where we could camp free and managed to arrange work for all the men trimming Christmas trees on the other side of town, for which we would each be paid 1.75 dollars an hour (14s7d). The farm also included huge areas of grape vines. It was run by Korky and Ierene Kevorski and their three children.

The first day was a Saturday. We started at about 11am and my diary records 'we were exhausted by 12.30. Very, very hot, machetes and shears, filthy work and bitten badly. We have to trim trees to about eight feet in height, and the right shape. That night we slept outside, badly, despite being very tired.'

The following day we started work at 6.20am and Don, Roger and I finished at 4pm, whilst the others preferred to finish at 12 and then work from 4pm to 8pm, all of which meant the bus had to make annoying journeys between the river and the workplace, six in all, and as we cook late the bus doesn't cool down. We slept outside at night.

As often happened when we were not on the road, some tensions crept in, mostly about who was working hardest, and why we had to cook so late, and my diary recorded: 'Half the bus are not on good terms. On Monday, Don, Rog and I managed two and a half rows of Christmas tree cutting as well as an interview for a newspaper and a radio station, while Bob, Mike and Dave did two rows in the morning, and thought we should have done more.'

The girls discovered a pile of rotting fruit on Bob's old bunk (guess where he was?) which had to be thrown away.

On the Tuesday we finished over 3,000 Christmas trees and while some of the team spent the rest of the day lopping off the tree tops, I went with Korky's 16-year-old son Steve to pick up some new grape boxes from a local box company. It took some time to get them packed because they kept falling off the trailer.

The Kevorskis had had a rush order for grapes and had employed a team of Mexicans to pick them. They did 179 boxes from 6am to 5pm, which was regarded as very slow.

My diary recorded: 'As they are not allowed to lid or load the boxes, Antonio (a happy drunk Mexican), Steve and I, lid, label and put them on the trailer. It is very hot. There's ice-cold water in a barrel.

'Antonio has been here three years and yet can only speak two or three English words. He drives the trailer like a crazy man, tearing down the lines of vines, with us bumping along on the back trying to unload new boxes under the grapes without crushing them under the wheels. Quite a laugh really!'

128

On a more serious note, a surprise visit by local union officials upset the applecart – with both Antonio and I not being members of the union, not to mention working illegally. We had to keep out of sight. I took him deep into the rows of vines and kept him occupied spreading out boxes to his heart's content. I'm sure he didn't know what was going on.

Steve and I worked a 12-hour day and afterwards relaxed with a swim and a barbecue, during which Shelley, one of the daughters, very attractive, read my palm.

The whole team worked well; Mike was so tired he fell asleep driving a tractor and Bob had to shout to wake him up! We made 409 dollars for our graft, plus a bottle of brandy. and our spirits improved considerably!

The following day we headed north, across flat mostly arable land, cotton, corn, a few cows, a small wooden schoolhouse, a church with a bell tower. It was cool and relaxing in the bus.

We reached San Francisco late afternoon and parked at the docks to visit the Consul. Alcatraz, a collection of old iron on an island, shimmered across the water. Low cloud – a permanent feature, lay across the top of the city, cutting skyscrapers in half.

I had five letters. 'I have a nephew, David, brown hair' my diary recorded. 'Visited Fisherman's Wharf – looks and smells like a fishy English resort, Great Yarmouth maybe. The bus is making alarming noises in the area of the rear brakes. Consul people seem OK. Temperature here about 56F – there's a 20-degree difference from one side of the bay to the other, about eight miles. Feels very cold, and everyone dresses warmly to go out in the evening. It's a three dollar pay day!' I bet I blew it in one go.

Next day we headed for the State capital, Sacramento, to meet Governor Ronald Reagan, who had apparently shown interest in meeting us as a result of Senator Stephens' intervention.

We left San Francisco over the Bay Bridge, passing just under a couple of low bridge spans. The second gear was giving us trouble as well as the brakes, but we arrived at Sacramento just after midday and Roger and I met some officials from the permit office.

Bad news – they said they could not extend our permit beyond August 31. 'If we did we would be setting a precedent, we have already extended what we usually do. Normally an excess height vehicle would have been sent back to where it came from,' they said.

We can see their point, but think they should be more flexible. Roger told them that we had a very safe vehicle and every bit of wood that went into the interior was weighed so that there would be equal weight distribution. Not sure that was true!

All this meant we would have to be out of the state by August 30th and lose grape picking money.

We popped into the Capital Building, roomy and comfortable, white dome, and met Mrs Stephens, who had a look around the bus. Then we drove to a park near the river for the night. The next few days became quite hectic.

First, there were the essential repairs to the bus. The second gear would not hold in place, which could make life very difficult for the bus and us.

There were visits to the Capital to see the Senators in action on the final day of business. Senator Stephens gave a brief history of our travels and problems with permits with which he had assisted us.

We also shook hands with Governor Reagan, who would later become President of the United States. Our meeting ran over time and caused his aides some concern. He reminisced about his time in London and wished us well. 'He was wearing a big, square, suit, and looked tired. Very suntanned,' I wrote.

"He might have been nice when he was younger," said Sal.

It was a busy day for the Governor and he was about to leave for a flight south. He said he was pleased to see us (and a group of Explorer Scouts who shared the audience) and was interested in our trip.

Senator Stephens told him we were all from Bristol, except Bob who was from the Isle of Wight, although in fact it was me who was the sole Wightman! Mr Reagan said he was in London last Fall and had made a film at Elstree.

Senator Stephens had been able to get us a 4-day extension to our permit. He later took us to his apartment complex, where we made use of the swimming pool before returning to Miller Park. We had a visit from the local police who were very pleasant and they later came back with lots of fresh fruit for us.

Our next visitor was Davy Crockett and his daughter. They had a tour of the bus and later he took Mike and me to his house for a beer.

Dave recorded that the bus had travelled just five miles that day, making a total of 7,576 miles since we started.

In the evening we were visited by the Vice Squad, patrolmen Dan Anderson and Jerry Morin, of police unit 4, who brought with them some peaches and cantaloupes, and showed us a Magnum 357 Colt six-shot. "If we have got to use them, then we want to be able to stop anything," said Jerry. The gun would stop a car. A mate, a cop, was shot dead a few weeks before, aged 24. They also had mace gas.

Police cars have no rear door handles, and no protection from bullets. They received a message about three armed men, so they left. Four more cops visited at about 11.15pm, another one at 5am next day, and several others through the day.

Stories in the Sacramento Union mentioned the police had said they would help us in any way they could.

We found the police generally very helpful on our travels, although once out of North America the language barrier caused some misunderstanding.

One thing I noticed was that there wherever we went there were lots of police, far more than in the UK where you seldom see an officer.

Some might argue that's a good thing, because it indicates less crime and more freedom here, but I found it reassuring to see police as we travelled.

The ones we met in the USA and Canada certainly had the same dark humour as you get with UK police and other emergency services as an escape from the harsh realities of what they and the other emergency services have to cope with.

I give you two home-grown examples – a police sergeant rang me at the Sheffield Star to give me an update on a witness appeal, and having been put through by the friendly switchboard girl, he said "As I was just saying to your accomplice..."

Then there was the time my ambulanceman friend, Graham, and his colleague were sent out to help a man who had reportedly tried to cut his throat and then had second thoughts.

As the tearful man was being loaded into the back of the ambulance, he asked them: "How bad does it look?" To which Graham's colleague replied: "Well, I'll put it like this – I wouldn't nod your head."

Sal liked a man in uniform. In a letter home, she wrote: 'In the police station there's a notice about us, saying we are OK – not hippies – and to keep an eye on us and make sure we are alright.

'We have had cops here day and night; the other morning there were eight of them at one time. They are absolutely great! They came round when we were having a meal, found out that we had no fruit and on their next visit bought us a bag of peaches and cantaloupes. Even had the vice squad visit – interesting finding out how they work.'

We needed to carry out repairs to the gear box and this involved raising the bus some four feet off the ground. Don and I collected some packing wood to support the bus from a Salvation Army hostel, and the lads spent a hard day working on it. They fixed the rear brake (nearside) with a temporary rubber ring and worked on the second gear, but without much success.

A local couple entertained us to a barbecue, and a woman fishing nearby with her husband said she would never send her children to state schools because they were run on political lines, yet she worked for the education department!

Roger and Bob carried on trying to get the bus fixed, but it was too much for them. The Bee carried a story headlined 'Buss on a busted bus' which described our problems, and also highlighted some improvements we wished we had included before we started off, like having an air conditioner – "it was beastly hot in Mexico" we were quoted as saying, although I bet none of us had ever used the word in our lives – and a generator, to keep us in power no matter what.

Dave recorded: 'Saturday 22 August 1970: Today we began to sort out the bus mechanical problems. The brakes were taken apart and reassembled. There was no obvious fault and they sounded a bit better. The gearbox presents a bigger problem. The normal exit route for the gearbox is via a maintenance hatch in the floor of the bus into the main cabin.

'This is not possible because of the conversion so we are going to have to lift the bus up quite high.

'Senator Stephens came to the rescue again, suggesting we try the Motor Inn Commercial Garage, and they sent a Greek mechanic and a much-improved jack with which the gearbox was a lot more accessible.

It turned out that a ring had lost its temper, probably because of the heat. A local university has four double-deckers, and they ask if we need any spares.'

Patrolman Jerry Moran invited us to his house. His wife, Irma, and four children were there. He had a nice pool and we had a BBQ. It was due to end about 7pm, but we were all having so much fun it went on until 2am!.

The following day we were taken to a restaurant by Darlene Christoni. We were then taken to the California State Fair and presented with VIP tickets. This gave us free rides on all the activities.

Dave's diary recorded: 'Tuesday 25 August 1970 - We got back to the bus in the morning and it had had to be jacked up to an even more precarious angle to slide the gearbox out. It was taken to a transmission shop for examination. The good news is that the fault is a simple one. The circlip that holds the gear in place had sprung loose allowing the gear to slip along the shaft. It just needed being put back.

'This must be a known fault as once it was found an examination of the gear housing revealed an access panel that can get at these clips.

'If it goes again we will need to crawl under the bus and fiddle around as our interior modifications make it difficult. In the evening we went to the home of the garage owner, Nino, for dinner. He waived all charges for their work and gave us a $10 donation.

'Wednesday 26 August 1970. - Borrowed Nino's pick-up truck and Roger and I went to the transmission shop to collect the gearbox.

'The foreman gathered all his workers around the box to show it off to them. He enthused about the quality of workmanship and told his workers they were unlikely to see the like again. They waived all charges for work done.'

With the bus uninhabitable, we were farmed out to the homes of fellow Bristolians we had met, Vic and Barbara King and Bert Terry, a former Western Daily Press reporter, and his sister, and I got a wet ear and a soaked bed when the sprinkler system turned on accidentally. Stop smoking that stuff in bed!

Dave's diary: 'Thursday 27 August 1970 - Work commenced on getting the gearbox back under the bus and ready to hoist. It is a long and laborious job, but by mid-afternoon it was in position and all that remains is to reconnect everything and tighten it all up. We were taken out for a boat ride in the afternoon. It was very relaxing. The TV crew came back for another story.

'Friday 28 August 1970: Roger and Bob did the main work on the gearbox with John and me assisting and doing other odd jobs around the bus.'

Don and Mike managed to get a job cleaning the condemned kitchens at a local restaurant. The rest of us pottered about doing little jobs and I contacted some more newspapers and TV stations, and we also managed to get some cheap clothes from the Veterans Thrift Shop; I had some cut-down shorts for 25cents! Darlene Christoni and her husband, Tom, were very good, providing lifts for Don and Mike to the restaurant and putting up four of us overnight. They also gave us clothes… and a thank you card to send her!

We were featured on two TV stations and after each appearance we are inundated with visitors, several bringing goodies, like food, beer etc. Jerry Marin, invited us to a party, said phone him when we were ready to go, so he could pick us up, and gave me 20 cents to make the phone call! That's hospitality!

Local police visited us again, and explained how to get jobs picking fruit without permits on 8th street, between 1 and 5pm!

However, we had in the short term found work; all hands to the pumps at the restaurant, the Chandelier, a clean up to satisfy health inspectors. We started work at 11pm, cleaning up all the fat and the filthy fridge. By early morning we were tired out, all for two dollars an hour each. We stopped for Mike's breakfast and then carried on, and on, until 5pm, 18 hours non-stop. Next day we had off, but back to work on the Sunday, from 10am until 5pm.

We earned 322 dollars and also received a collection from grateful customers. The restaurant was back in business!

We now had 1,120 dollars in the kitty, and loads of donated food and clothes. One night we saw a weird light in the sky, travelling fast with a great beam, which seemed to explode and vanish.

It turned out to be a NASA rocket that had gone off course and was deliberately blown up.

On August 31, the date our permit expired, Roger went to see Senator Stephens' secretary. The Highways Department extended our permits to September 25 and included Fresno. We also managed to fix up a permit for Oregon, and had a useful new contact, a Federal senator in Washington DC. We rang Korky and he said we would have all the work we wanted.

The people of Sacramento had been extremely helpful and generous; we managed to get a new 20-ton jack worth $120 for half that price, and a new grease gun for $3. So many people had donated food that we have to be careful not to mention we needed anything, because they went off and got it! Strawberry wine, popcorn, steaks, and lots of other delights.

Several of our new friends arrived to say goodbye the following day. My diary read: 'It's rather sad, really, but we have had to get used to saying our goodbyes to people and places. Another chapter ends.'

CHAPTER 12

We headed for San Francisco and parked at Fisherman's Wharf. The six lads got ready and went out for the evening, Broadway, China Town, Market Street, filthy book shops, garish lights, kinky strip joints. We ended up at the Red Garter bar, where we bought some drinks, and had some bought for us. Sally returned from a few days break in San Diego; it took her nine hours to hitch back.

Roger and I had an appointment with Bruce of Sta-Power in San Rafael , and we took a Greyhound bus, at a dollar each. We went across the bridge that spans the Golden Gate entrance to the bay, with great views from the Sausolito side despite the fog.

We visited the Sta-Power offices to learn he was not in until the next day, and saw 'God' from a distance. We also met the woman in charge of advertising, who seemed quite impressed and asked for a contact phone number in case he turned up. We said "c/o the bus station!"

However, as we wandered around we met an English colonial type, who gave us a lift to the police station, and there we met a former Bristol woman, who was thrilled by our story and persuaded the police chief to find us a motel for the night, paid for by the Salvation Army.

This is the area where a judge was kidnapped from his court room and shot a few weeks before, and the five kidnappers were in turn shot and killed by police as they fled in a car. The police took us to the motel and the receptionist eyed the two of us and said suspiciously: "Do you want a double or two singles?"

It was a dead town, but the police fixed up an evening with the local Mayor which was very pleasant.

The rest of the bus crew departed San Francisco for Fresno shortly after being presented with six large cases of Guinness by a local rep.

Bruce hadn't arrived at Sta-Power HQ the following day, but was apparently heading for the Sheridan Palace Hotel in San Francisco. So we hitched there to check. He arrived at about 4pm with some excuse or other; we presumed he had just forgotten us. He said he would talk to 'God' about us. We get the feeling even divine intervention won't help us get any Sta-Power cash.

My diary continued: 'So there I am in the foyer of the Sheridan Palace Hotel, wondering where we should go for the night as it was too late to hitch to Fresno, when out of nowhere appeared the parents of Chris, the girl I met in San Diego! What a co-incidence! They gave us the address of a woman who had been very helpful once before, and she says we can stay the night in her apartment (on the floor). We took the 25-cent ferry to Sausalito with her. Sausalito feels like home, old stone harbour wall, quaint streets of shops and restaurants, very misty!

'Next morning we hitched down to Fresno – the last lap by Highway Patrol. We had run out of lifts and Roger decided to flash his international police association membership card at the Highway patrol HQ to see if they could help. Turned out they had been told about us anyway, and after allowing us to sit-in on a briefing they drove us back. I hoped they didn't smell the funny fag fumes from my pipe! We got back at about 7.30pm.'

The rest of the bus crew had been trimming grapes for two days, 10 hours a day, making 280 dollars. But Korky then flooded the fields, so for a couple of days we had time to relax and enjoy more hospitality.

Manuel Radael and Richard Dressler took us to beautiful Yosemite national park for a day, and someone else took us water skiing.

140

Roger was soon on his feet, Bob also, but Jan, Ripper and I struggled and eventually were so cold we had to pack it in.

However, the following day Mike got up as well! A triumph in these hard times! September 7 was Labour Day, a national holiday, so more relaxing!

A TV crew filmed us and it was arranged that we should go on the Jim Collins Nite Call show the following day, after a full day in the fields stripping leaves from around bunches of grapes, and turning them over to the sunny side. Sal, Joan, Roger and I did the talk-in, answering questions from the compere and the public for two and a half hours.

One listener questioned why we didn't have an air conditioning unit with us when we started the trip, and became quite abusive, and then several other people rang in to apologise for him. I was obviously quite impressed with it all, for my diary recorded: 'It was a really good show and Jim is a nice fellow, aged about 28, who says he is trying to get out of the rat race of local radio. I think this type of show would go down well in England.'

The following day we were up at 6am for another day's grind, temperature in the 100s. Roger sprained his ankle and went back to our base and while laid up managed to fix up two lectures for school kids at $25 a time.

That night we had a bit of a row about whether the front window should be left open or not, and the following morning we stayed in bed late as there were only nine rows of vines left to do at Korky's, which took us about 90 minutes. Some of us went to a Country and Western evening with Jim Collins, and Roger phoned up the Nite Call show to reply to a woman, who had rung in criticising England.

My diary read: 'Heard there was an earthquake in LA, not very serious. Got some large self-tappers (screws) for the bunks which are coming away from the side of the bus along 'screw alley.' Tonight a dust storm blew up and the temperature cooled.'

We had a fire in the bus. A wooden rubbish box caught fire for no apparent reason, and the flames took hold of the Formica covering the butane gas hatch. Bernice threw the box out and smothered the hatch fire. We realised we needed a fire extinguisher and to be more careful about matches and smoking.

Anyone trapped on the top deck would have had little chance of escape from a serious fire in the kitchen area as the rear stairs would have become quickly engulfed. If fire had broken out, say in the middle of the night, would we have made a dash for it without a second thought? Or grabbed some vital possessions?

Years later my wife, Nancy, and I were staying on the 16th floor of a hotel in Sydney when the fire alarm went off just after midnight. What was my priority? To get out? To grab my wife and get out? To grab my underpants and my wife? What about my wallet and my teeth in the glass next to the bed (I'm joking about the teeth).

In fact I grabbed at my underpants, attempted to put both legs through one leg of my jeans, fell over, pulled them on, grabbed my wallet and followed my wife out of the door. She, by the way, had miraculously managed to become fully dressed and looked quite fashionable. The corridor was full of Chinese guests in Calvin Kline underpants. Are they made in China? Anyway, it was a false alarm.

Back at the bus Dave's diary recorded a dramatic moment: 'Sunday 13 September 1970 - Mike obtained some larger skis from the store and we tried again. This was a far better day as Mike can now get up out of the water. By the end of the day he was quite confident and even tried to ski on one foot. This ended in a spectacular fall in the water. I have also become more proficient but fell over when I tried one foot skiing.'

But Dave said that while lounging around at lunchtime he noticed a young girl who seemed to be in difficulty in the water. He mentioned it to Mike, who took one look and then sped across the grass and dived in.

He swam to the girl and then brought her back to the shore.

Well done, Mike! And my story about his bravery made the Bristol Evening Post back home.

Bristol man saves American girl

by JOHN WINTER

A Bristol man has rescued a young girl from drowning in California.

He swam out and pulled her back to shore, where she was recovered by a grateful mother.

okay but she panicked and let go of a rubber tyre she was clinging to."

The same stretch of river

We had a tour of the Sun Maid raisin factory, the biggest in the world, where our dried grapes went. The raisins arrive all dirty from the fields in trucks and can be cleaned and sorted and boxed in 20 minutes! We tried to get jobs for a week, and then to get advertising, but the best they could do was offer free raisins all over the USA in return for two six-foot advertisements on the side of the bus. I hate raisins anyway. It was raisins all the way that day, we ended up rolling raisins into paper for Lindy; four of us were paid 35 dollars for two hours' work.

Dave's records revealed the bus had travelled 8,566 miles since it landed in Montreal four months before.

Dave, Mike, Bob and I stayed behind in Fresno when the bus went back to San Francisco to make another attempt to get a marketing deal with Sta Power.

We had borrowed a tent from a friend at Reedley, Richard Dressler. Mike cooked over an open fire, so every day someone had to get up at 5am to get the fire going with wood and paper we kept in the tent to keep it dry from the overnight dew, and to prepare smoked tea and toast.

On two or three nights we were woken by scavenging dogs outside, and Bob woke up Mike once to get him to shoo them away!

This time we were working in an orchard of almond trees. We were up at 6am before the sun was up, and didn't get back until the sun had gone down again. A ten-hour working day banging almond trees with hammers, ducking the falling nuts because they really stung, and then collecting them together so they could be shovelled into big bins. It was back-breaking work.

The first day one of the workers showed us what to do, banged the tree with a hammer. and Mike retreated under a hail of falling nuts. I went to the first tree, gave it a sharp bang, and one nut fell off!

Dave remembered it thus: 'Wednesday 16 September - Monday 21 September 1970 - We were up at 05.00 hrs and away at 06.00 hrs. Arrived at 07.00hrs and started work. You spread some sacking around the tree to catch the nuts and then one brave person, we took it in turns, moved in to stand by the trunk.

'Lifting a rubber mallet the trunk was dealt a hard blow that set up a big vibration through the trunk and branches. A split second after hitting the trunk the almonds hit you back as they fell off the branches. Hats were worn to reduce the impact on the head.

'We found a tree with a rather large hornet's nest in it. The hornets were rather angry when disturbed and we had no way of getting rid of them, so a cluster of four trees was left unpicked. However we finished off the rest of the orchard and returned to the river.'

We were paid 12 and a half dollars a bin. We did over 30 bins and collected 430 dollars for a week's work. We would get back to the tent covered in dust and very, very tired, have a shower, finish cooking the meal in the dark, and go to bed at about 8pm! Eventually we finished work earlier so we could see what we were eating.

One night we were woken at 2am by shouting. The farm boss, John Ugaste, and his rather large girl friend, Myrtle, had arrived for a chat.

They were both a little tipsy. We reluctantly crawled out of our sleeping bags to meet her, except for Dave who grumpily refused until the towering Myrtle went into the tent after him. Seconds later, asked what he was doing, he said: "Entertaining this charming young lady." The couple left after a little persuasion.

After six days work at Reedley we said goodbye to the Lindholmes, who had been very good to us, and went to the Greyhound stadium at Fresno to catch the bus back to San Francisco, where the rest of the crew were. Our mattresses and sleeping bags followed us on a raisin lorry to a city market, where we eventually tracked them down at 2am in the morning. I had been up for 22 hours.

Reunited with the others at our bus the good news was that we had 2,000 dollars in the kitty. While they were in San Francisco, the rest of the crew had been flogging horse brasses and earning 60 dollars a day for parking outside Roos-Atkins during their Euro Fair week.

Sally and Jan had been busy working on attracting jewellery orders. The Sta-Power project had fallen through, but we were pursuing Guinness to see if they would give us funding to travel to Australia. The city was full of the noise of wailing fire engines, turning out to fight forest fires bordering a district where many wealthy people lived, destroying 40 homes.

Thursday, September 22 was the day my dad had a hip operation. We kept in regular touch by letter, but it made me feel a very long way away. We left Sausalito at about 6.10am driving north towards Oregon along the 101.

It was a delightful drive through redwood forests, alongside the River Eel for some distance. The Avenue of the Giants was particularly impressive, towering tree trunks disappearing into the sky.

It was getting colder and when we stopped at Rio Dell to shop a local said there would be too much snow for us to cross the Rockies soon. Most of the locals work at the Pacific Lumber Company. My diary read: "Roast pork and ice cream for dinner, we are living well!"

Early next day we arrived at Humbolt Bay, a glimpse of white surf through the trees, then 100 yards of brush and a beach covered in redwood driftwood. It was the coldest water I have ever paddled in; my feet went numb after a minute.

My diary reads: 'Lost second gear again. Bob and Roger worked under the bus for one and a half hours and replaced a split ring but we may have to get a new one.'

CHAPTER 13

We crossed the border into Oregon at about 5.30pm and parked on a pleasant spot by a harbour, tree-covered hill all around, salmon in the river, squadrons of herons that dive down into the water followed by hundreds of screaming seagulls scavenging for bits. The birds hang around for fishing boats to return and then follow them in. Apparently thousands of dead anchovies were washed up here recently because of a lack of oxygen in the river, and the birds had a great time.

This was Brookings, a town of about 2,000 people, many retired, most of the employment in the saw mills and lumber business and in fishing.

We saw a school of anchovies so large that they turned the green water black, with thousands of gulls diving into the breakers to get at them. Huge numbers of the fish were hurling themselves on to the beach, possibly pursued by larger predators, and we joined locals in collecting bucketfuls of them. I recorded: 'The gulls on the beach are like a party of elderly schoolmistresses, strutting anxiously around and running like hell when the sea comes lapping up at their feet.'

I rang the local radio station to tell them who we were, and they asked me if we were Christians. Of course!

Dozens of people started to arrive to have a look at us. We sold about $20 of horse brasses and Charlie from the radio station came down and took Jan and Bob off fishing; they caught several sea trout.

Many people said they had heard us on San Francisco radio and two sweet middle-aged ladies came up from Crescent City after hearing my interview. The good news was that there might be some lily bulbs to pick if the weather cooled – too warm, and the bulbs would split. There was also a chance we might be able to pack prawns at the cannery (remove their tails).

Lee, the lily farm host, who occasionally hikes inland to shoot elk, cut down some overhanging branches on trees next to his yard, so the bus could get in, but it was still too big.

The locals were friendly; they told us that this was the only state on the North American continent to be bombed in the Second World War. A plane launched from a Japanese sub dropped incendiary bombs that started a few fires, and further inland a balloon dropped a bomb that killed two picnickers.

Roger and Bob spent the next two days working on the bus and arranging permits whilst the rest of us worked in the lily bulb fields, either planting them, or picking them. It's fairly light work, but means lots of bending. And it was boring! We relieved the tedium (accidentally) by driving over two full boxes in the pick-up truck (Ripper) and overturning four others spilling all the bulbs (me).

Apparently after the lily bulblets are picked off the stems they are transported East and stored at 40F, then taken out after a few weeks and placed in greenhouses at 60F, to be ready for sale in their pots at Easter.

Sally worked in the bulb-measuring sheds, grading them. Of the six women working with her, three had been separated or divorced, all had two or more children, and all were married by the age of 18! There were toilet huts everywhere in the fields for the convenience of workers – 'they stood every hundred yards or so, like lonely sentry boxes' I recorded. It was dusty work, particularly when the wind sprang up.

Someone told us that the town had 21 churches, not bad for such a small population. It was also said that a group of locals were facing court charges after shaving the hair off the heads of some hippies a few miles north. We had better keep up our appearances!

My diary read: 'This is quite a religious area, but not very tolerant. Charlie told us that they move hippies on if they try and stay in town. We were entertained to a barbecue in the evening, followed by a vicar's tea party, which ended with us all holding hands. There are not many young people around, they must be away at college. It's a bit dull here.'

We were told we could work in the lily fields for up to a month, and Don and Mike also went up in to the hills and picked apples. They found a racoon with its leg caught in a trap and the man with them released it by cutting the leg off.

There were Russian trawlers off the coast; apparently whenever the fog came down they moved inside the 12-mile limit to poach some fish. They were much bigger and faster than the local boats.

Roger, Bern, Don and I went to the Sporthaven Inn, Chetco River, and enjoyed some beer and a sausage and mash dinner, in friendly company. Sally was still on a diet, my diary recorded.

There was some difference of opinion on whether to stay around for a month and work in the lily bulbs or move on to Canada and take a chance on finding work there. Another option was two weeks in Brookings and a couple more on the apple plantation at the Hook River, which seemed a good compromise.

In retrospect I'm not convinced returning to Canada was ever a good idea, as we could have turned back through the USA, hopefully finding work on our way, and then resumed our journey to South America and onwards.

We knew crossing Canada in the depths of winter would be difficult, but it was always part of the plan - maybe we hoped to make a lot of money in Vancouver. Anyway, it was probably a naive decision.

We were all short of shoes, so Roger agreed that we should have ten dollars each to buy some. We also bought a second-hand generator for $150.

The Sportshaven Inn was the place that saw the most action. Don, Jan, Bob, Sal and I went in one evening and although it was quiet at first, it soon livened up. It was the first day of the deer hunting season and several hunter's wives came in to let their hair down, as well as several divorcees. On another occasion I saw two fist-fights and the Sheriff arrived, baton in hand, holster unbuttoned.

We worked a couple of days in the fields for our own pockets, and on another day one of the bosses complained about our work and said Don and I had done nothing all day. He later apologised after I threatened to quit and said the dust had got to him, and when we left he said it had been a pleasure to work with us!

My diary recorded: 'I have three clean odd socks, all the rest are dirty, so Dave lent me a pair of his. Met two of Sal's new friends, Hippy Gene and John, who live in a house they call a sewer, where they have beer cans hanging down on string instead of curtains.

'We all went to Tubby's restaurant as had been arranged with 'Tubby' for free dinners, but no-one knew a 'Tubby' although they thought it might have been the manager, so we had the steak meals! I went to the Sportshaven to meet a girl who didn't turn up, but instead a most delightful Mexican-Indian girl, known as Mex for short, invited me to sit with her and her boyfriend, and we had a very nice evening. My English accent was obviously working miracles again - a drunk shook hands with me five times in ten minutes wishing me the best of luck!"

With a little money to spend, the single members of the crew were able to get out and socialise. My diary recorded: 'At one time I was by myself in the bus with the Coles and the Pooles and both couples were rowing.

So as I couldn't go upstairs or downstairs to get away from them, I went out. I got back at 5am, Dave 6am, Mike 9.30am and Sal at 11.30am!'

The lads finished working on the generator and we were able to spend some evenings in the bus under the flickering lights it generated. But it was getting towards the middle of October, and, worried about the weather deteriorating, we decided it was time to move on again. We had a generous send-off from people we had met at Brookings and drove off along the coast road, massive rocks as big as houses on the beach, tree-covered hills. The generator then packed in!

We made good time along the 101, surrounded by wonderful scenery, leaves turning brown and red, passed the huge Coos Bay bridge, one of several where we drove in the middle of the road to make sure we squeezed under the overhead gantries. At Salem we hit the overhead traffic lights but no serious damage.

We made our way to the Capitol Building to meet the Governor, Tom McCall, at 6ft 5inches the tallest Governor in the States (he probably had to duck under the swinging traffic lights), a former journalist.

He was a very amiable fellow – he looked at the bus from his balcony, asked if we were musicians and wanted us to sing! Obviously a fan of Summer Holiday. He joked about everything. We all posed for photos before parking overnight next to a railroad shunting yard. That sort of summed us up, one minute mixing with the rich and powerful in luxurious surroundings, the next relegated to the railway sidings!

Apparently there had been some bombings in Rochester, New York and on the West Coast by the Weatherman group of young extremists, protesting about 'the system.'

We hadn't heard about it and were, in fact, out of touch with world or even national affairs as we had no TV or radio and seldom bought a newspaper.

Of course, you can't believe all you read in newspapers anyway – for example, have I told you about my work as an astrologer? No, well, here goes. I can't recall which newspaper it was, one of the weeklies that I worked on, but the practice was to use one of the reporters to do the Your Life in the Stars column each week, and that became my job. I had to go back 10 years into the files of the paper and copy the Your Life in The Stars entry for the corresponding week.

If I thought they were gloomy forecasts I would brighten them up a bit, and I sometimes I asked my fellow employees for their star sign and gave them an especially good one!

So be warned!

We went window shopping and I discovered a great pipe shop, Treasure Pipes, where they blended their own baccy. It sold pipes of all shapes. The owner said he had trouble getting big pipes from England. The Yanks only smoked big pipes, partly because tobacco is so much cheaper over there.

We drove to Portland and stayed at the Ramada Inn, the best hotel in town. Well, we were in the car park behind the best hotel in town. Some of the guests were probably surprised to see Sal running in with a saucepan to fetch some water; we had run out again.

Don, Mike and myself went into town to see if we could see any nightlife. We had heard that there were six women to every man in the city. In one seedy bar we asked the barman where there was any action, and he wrote something down and handed us a folded note. Two addresses. "Thanks" we grinned, and wondered what we were getting into.

One was a coffee bar that was empty. We carried on down dark and dismal streets passed a few leering prostitutes (we leered back) and came to a building with gyrating figures painted on the walls and music emanating from within. We went inside and ordered drinks, looked round at a topless figure dancing to music on a shelf in the corner – and it was a bloke. A waiter arrived: "Yes, dears, what would you like?" We ordered three beers, drank quickly and left. We had entered a gay bar by mistake.

We visited a shopping centre that was said to be the largest in the world, with an ice-skating rink in the middle, and Mike discovered he could get pork at 38 cents a pound compared to 72 cents back home in England.

We left early the following morning aiming for the apple orchards of the Hood River, through hilly countryside alongside the Colombia river, Roger and I clambered up the rocks alongside the 600-foot Mulinomah Falls, spray everywhere, water thundering as it hit the pool below. We were drenched!

When we arrived at the Hood River, we were told the fruit harvesting season was almost over, but a cute little traffic warden (we don't get many of them in the UK, they are usually big and hairy) passed on the word that we were looking for work and within a few hours a farmer had driven in from six miles out of town to offer us all jobs, for a week.

We started at 3pm and by 6pm had only filled just over five bins with apples (at $5.50 a bin). Slow work. We had the use of a little house with a toilet, radio (we hadn't seen a TV for months, apart from cadging a look after we were interviewed) and grotty bedrooms.

The work was OK. I always liked climbing trees, and these weren't huge ones. But we had to wait for the frost to rise before we could start, so it held us up.

One morning quite early a couple arrived to say they had seen a report about us in the Oregon Journal. The woman was very nice but her husband – who seemed to be drunk - was quite rude, suggesting we were spongers and layabouts. His wife was upset and refused to drive their car, so he did, roaring off in a rage, straight into a ditch! It nearly went into the river. We strolled over, surveying the problem, and then used a truck to haul him out. He was a bit embarrassed.

That evening we were invited to the local Elk Club by Sam Galloway, a local historian, and enjoyed free beer and crab. Spongers? No, we were just grateful for the generosity shown to us.

In a letter home I said: 'There are a lot of very religious people in these small towns. Don made us laugh when we watched this chap trying to get his tractor started, by saying "Oh Lord, give me the power and deliverance to make this bloody tractor work".'

I had seen quite a lot of Mex (or Ermenia, her real name) in Brookings and she was obviously interested in joining us on the rest of the trip, which would bring the crew back to its original size.

She worked as a nanny at a house overlooking the river estuary and her boss shot seals from his veranda with a rifle. She was quite wild herself, having once "rode the trains" – i.e. jumped on slow-moving freight trains and travelled across country on them.

One morning when we couldn't work because it was raining, we had a talk amongst ourselves and decided it was not practical for her to join us. I later realised it would have been a disaster.

Soon after we resumed work that afternoon, the boss, Rolf Smiley, rushed up and said: "There's steam coming out of the bus, what do I do?" Dave had left the kettle on. Crisis quickly over; a slightly singed kettle.

Don then drove the bus into a slight collision with a house, bending one of our panels. We made a hasty exit; slightly singed pride.

We did well picking the red apples, filling four boxes an hour, but when they ran out Smiley wouldn't let the men pick the golden delicious as we were too rough with them. The girls had a gentler touch. But it meant we had half the crew not earning money.

We were all very amused to watch a drunken horse staggering around in a neighbouring field after eating too many fallen apples, including some we lobbed over to him – apparently they turn to alcohol in a horse's stomach. "As pissed as a horse…"

In the Oregonian newspaper, I was quoted as recalling the first day of our trip when "everyone got up and came downstairs to wash at the same time. It was ridiculous. Now if you hear someone else get up you stay in bed for a few more minutes."

And Roger commented:" We learn more living this way in a week that you would in two years living a normal life. When you get in trouble you have to figure a way to get out of it."

The US economy at that time – and probably now – depended heavily on immigrant labour, illegal or not. We had a good example of this when Don had to have another injection of Vitamin B12 to help clear up his eye infection, and Smiley generously took us into town to the doctor. He was, he told us, chairman of the county Republican party, and sometimes toured with Governor McCall.

Three of his Mexican workers were picked up by a highway patrolman for being illegal immigrants. It left him short-handed and threatened to disrupt his business. So he complained to the boss. And as a result the officer was being moved out of state fast.

McCall was said to have told the State police chief: "You don't know what a Mexican looks like, do you…"

It was raining every day and after particularly heavy showers water would seep into the bus, not only through cracks in the roof, but along seams around the windows. The unwary sleeper would get a rude awakening when a stream of water hit them in the ear.

Roger and Bernice in the front, surrounded by leaking windows, were particularly badly affected by damp pillows and sleeping bags.

With the weather worsening and Smiley refusing to let the men work, maybe it was time for the bus to move on. It was time for a united front; we told him if the men couldn't earn money, then the girls wouldn't work either… and he said that was OK with him!

The aim was to drive up to Vancouver, across Canada, and back down to the fruit fields of the South, principally Florida, to raise more money to keep the trip going.

However, I would not be going with them. I had decided to have a month off with friends I had made in Brookings.

CHAPTER 14

My friends, Hippy Gene and his housemate, John, said they would be pleased to help me stay around for a month. I would be living with Hippy Gene at the Sewer Inn.

I wasn't sure what I would do for money, hopefully find work, nor how I would get back to the bus, but there had always seemed to be a solution to all the problems we encountered and I had the confidence of youth - everything would turn out fine. I liked the wild coast and forests of Oregon, the climate was a nice change from the searing heat of the Californian vineyards, and I was ready for a break from my companions.

The bus dropped me off at Portland on October 22 and I took a Greyhound bus back to Brookings, where a local police officer gave me a hard look as I alighted. I wasn't run out of town, so I must have passed inspection.

The bus headed north. Bernice wrote in her diary: 'This morning when Sally decided she didn't want me standing in her way, she plucked me off the floor, crushed my head against the ceiling and sat me down, humbly, in my seat. I didn't argue.'

Arriving in Seattle, they found to their horror that the roads were like San Francisco roller coasters. There was a letter from the British Embassy in Panama quoting $950 for the bus and passengers to go by boat from Panama to Colombia with Pacific Nord SA.

The bus was parked at the waterfront, and a cop turned up and said it would cost $4 for a permit every time the bus moved around the city. When he'd gone, Don told Bob to dump our rubbish bag in the water as it would sink. Bob did as was directed, and it didn't - "it bloody well just floated off" he remonstrated!

Back at Brookings, Hippy Gene and John were both carpenters and they said they could get me a job. They had an unusual working week; they would drink all day Saturday, Sunday and Monday whilst watching American college and professional football from dawn to dusk, and work like mad Tuesday, Wednesday and Thursday. On Fridays sometimes they worked and sometimes they drank. It was an appealing lifestyle after the serious hard work of the bus.

They let me stay without paying rent until I could earn some money. Eating was a new experience; the fridge was piled high with poached elk, and we even had venison burgers!

I wrote home: 'People are very kind here. I went into a bar to get a six-pack of beer the other evening, leaving Ermenia (Mex) outside in her car with the engine running, and when I started to talk and they heard my accent they all rushed over and shook hands, someone went out and brought Ermenia in, and someone else bought me two big packs of beer!'

More worryingly (for those at home) I continued: 'I have a job in house construction and live with two fellows in a house they call the Sewer Inn. They are both carpenters, so one day they just built a huge and quite elegant bar right across their living room. They are taking me deer hunting from a plane.'

Back at the bus they were waiting for Sal to return from a visit to a Great Aunt. She had been gone overnight. Don suggested they drag the river for her.

It turned out to be a busy day: Don and Bob failed to get a new carburettor for the generator and Roger arranged for TV and newspapers to visit, the idea being that maybe someone would offer under-cover accommodation for the bus so they could work on sealing all the leaks.

Sally arrived back with her relatives. She had phoned police to find out where the bus was and they told her it had been impounded! In fact, that was another, locally-owned bus, which had hit a bridge and caused some damage.

They had permission to sell some British hand bells, and they did well, only one out of eight were left. The crew were invited to an evening out at the Britannia Club. Bernice's diary recorded: 'Ever bump-started a double-decker? We had to tonight. The batteries were flat, so we all got in front and heaved it back down a slope. It started! Everyone was pretty sloshed, especially Don and Ripper who were dancing in the aisle.'

Jan and Bernice spent a lot of hours trying to get orders for Carbis jewellery from Seattle shopkeepers. The number of thrift shops encountered showed the depressed state of the city. 'We must be patriotic to tramp around all day for a few dollars,' she observed in her diary. But it proved a success, two orders worth $500. On one of the days they missed the local bus back and had to hitch two lifts and get a bus from a shopping centre They arrived just as the men were going out to search.

The snow-capped mountains surrounding the city were a constant reminder about the weather they might expect ahead of them in Canada, and on Wednesday, October 28th they crossed the border into Canada without any problem. The Customs officers didn't even look at the bus.

At Camas, near Vancouver, two local crafts people, Doris and Barry, provided some parchment scrolls and hangings which the crew agreed to sell. Barry was originally from Bradford, and their home was very British in style, even down to the piano, chime clock and horse brasses. On their return, the crew found the bus was leaking like a sieve, carpets soaked through upstairs and down. Mike later sold one of their paintings for $300 and Jan and Dave sold all the parchments!

There was a lot of British influence in Vancouver and that soon resulted in several orders for our British goods – jewellery, beer tankards, beefeater uniforms and fasteners. Mike was busily trying to sell the loos. Although the temperature was a mildish 39 degrees – Vancouver was sheltered by the mountains – the crew anticipated difficult conditions ahead and tried to get snow studs instead of chains for the wheels, but failed.

Halloween passed quietly, despite lots of local celebrations, and after obtaining the necessary permits the bus set off for Whistler Mountain through fantastic scenery, snow-capped mountains, tranquil lakes, pine forests, along steep, twisting roads. The ski lodge was disappointing, but three Gondola tickets were purchased at half-price and after a draw, Jan, Sally and Bernice apprehensively took the ride up the mountain.

At 6,000 feet they enjoyed great views, but stood out from the crowd in their everyday clothes, and made their way down by lift, passing the lads as they tried to walk up! There was a prospect of jobs in a few days, but next morning they returned to Vancouver. It was Cookie's birthday. 'The only thing anyone can think of getting him is chocolate digestive biscuits,' wrote Bernice.

Two or three firms showed interest in becoming agents for CPS Fasteners.

'We have heard today that England has had a mini-budget,' wrote Bernice. 'Fifty per cent of dental costs to be paid, prices of specs sky high, 1/6d on all prescriptions and you get the drugs you can afford to buy, and farmers subsidies taken off.'

On November 1 1970 Dave's diary records: 'Later Mike, Don, Sally and I had a long chat about our trip and how it is going. There is considerable dissatisfaction amongst the crew. There is concern about a lack of communication from Roger on any subject. Any matters raised are ignored.

'There has been no pay day since Brookings and though money is a constant worry, people need a bit of cash in their pockets. How and when problems will be resolved remains to be seen.'

Bernice wrote: 'We had a meeting where Dave decided he didn't like the way Roger was running things. It was decided, again, that a meeting should be held each week and $1 a week will be paid in wages. I will believe that when I see it!'

Just an aside, here, which may be relevant – I learned a lesson when I was quite young about trying to get individuals to do something together, when their natural instinct is to go their own way. When I was about 14, I was one of a group of about 30 lads and lasses who made little go-karts from old pram wheels and wooden boxes and used them to carry visitors' luggage from Sandown railway station to the hotels in the town.

In those days thousands of people, mostly families, travelled over on the ferry to Ryde each Saturday for their summer holidays, and took the steam trains to the Isle of Wight coastal resorts, Sandown, Shanklin and Ventnor. At Sandown we competed for their business with angry taxi drivers.

Some lads were bigger than others, and they managed to force their way through the melee to get the visitors' attention. So a couple of us decided to form a union, organise our labour, wait in turn (!) so that everyone would get a fair share of the business.

It was a disaster. The bigger lads refused to do it and while the rest of us waited in turn, they continued to steal the best jobs, targeting the richest-looking holidaymakers, the ones who would give the best tips, and we picked up the dregs. The union lasted one day!

Roger – who would later become Deputy General Secretary of NUPE and then UNISON and subsequently use his negotiating skills as chairman of the Parades Commission in Northern Ireland and in helping to settle the Post Office dispute in 2010-2012 - was the leader of the bus crew, as previously indicated, and found it was not easy to get a consensus about anything in a group of spirited individuals who wouldn't have been on the trip in the first place if they had wanted a quiet, uncomplicated, uncontroversial life.

He explained: 'We were all very young and at that age you don't have the experience of life to always be able to step back and see something from the other persons point of view. As a consequence I'm sure that I did not have the diplomatic skills I like to think I may have developed in later life. I am sure I rubbed people up the wrong way on occasions and they didn't have the skills necessarily to stand back either.

'Secondly we were living with and on top of one another 24/7. The meetings we used to have when we were away were not designed to find answers to problems, but to win arguments. The shortage of money and the unequal amounts we had taken away with us also contributed in my view to some of the anger that was on display on some occasions. There was also the factionalism that developed with some people talking to some but not others on occasions. I tried to keep away from that, but I'm sure I didn't succeed all the time.

'The disputes over things like should Mike do all the cooking, because he was the Chef, or should he (not unreasonably perhaps) have a day off from it from time to time became wearing at times. However on the whole it is probably amazing that a group of people who had very little in common at the outset not only got the bus converted, but got through all the bureaucracy and got away and stayed together as long as we did. It would be useful and interesting perhaps to get other people's thoughts on all of this.

'As we have said so many times a psychologist would have had a field day with us. Or they might have cracked under the strain of sharing the top deck of the bus with 10 others.'

Anyway, back to Canada. A Bristol émigré called Alexander Harrison employed Mike as chauffeur for his antique Rolls Royce. Mike bent the bumper on his first go at entering the garage, but Alex was OK about it and said he could have a Cadillac for his own personal use.

Bernice recorded: 'Some of us took the car through Stanley Park, and went across the Lions Gate Bridge to the Indian Reservation. Not a tepee in sight. They live in clapboard houses with polythene across the windows. Indians do not have the same rights as everyone else, which is rather unfair, as is the claim that they get drunk and smash glass windows!'

Back in Brookings I was living in the roof of the Sewer Inn, very cold and damp; you could see the sky through the shingles (like soft tiles)! I worked a couple of days on building a house, but was fired when I dropped a pack of shingles from the top of a ladder – I was very fit after months of physical work on a restricted diet, but just didn't have the strength, after scaling the ladder, to make the final step on to the roof!

My wages were soon spent - I bought some food and beer for the lads and had a crazy night at the Sportshaven Inn with the rest, breaking up a fight between two lumberjacks and, in turn, having to be restrained after a Mexican woman said: "The Queen is a whore".

I drove home (!) in a borrowed pick-up and ran over a skunk, the smell of which was sucked in by the air conditioning unit and made me feel sick.

I was actively looking for work, and through my housemates had made contact with a local eccentric, who had several businesses, a collection of hearses (for his personal pleasure) and a bi-plane, from which he bombed his house and those of his acquaintances with bags of flour. As you would!

He gave me two jobs – selling rhododendrons from a roadside stall, and filling in potholes on the drive of his home, which was miles from anywhere in dense woodland.

The first was a complete failure. I went on Radio Brookings and, in my English accent, urged people to stop and buy rhododendrons from me because: "I know all about them as I am English". A few people stopped, and I hardly sold any, probably due to the fact that I knew nothing about them at all, not even how to spell them, and if they asked: "Are they good in the shade?" I said they were, a similar answer to which I gave if they asked if they were good in direct sunlight. The road-digging job was cold and scary; I was alone, deep into bear country!

Back at the bus, the crew had accepted an invitation from the Bristol chap to go to a dance, which turned out to be a gathering of hippies and the people who helped them out, local social services and Salvation Army. Bernice reported: 'There was a crowd of half-nude hippies high on pot, which the place reeked of, as well as sweat, and they danced to bongo drums and bashed wooden blocks, and generally screamed. It's pitiful that they need to escape from the world this way.

'Then came a Salvation Army guitarist, who sang about the hippies being persecuted, and a preacher talking about why people dropped out, and a young chap who sang about the hypocrisy of the world.'

Sounded a fun do.

After further enquiries, it seemed that although four of the men would get jobs at Whistler Resort – Roger as a mechanic, the others on the Gondola – there was nothing for the girls, so it was decided that after further promotion work (already booked) and sorting out some travel arrangements the bus would carry on across Canada, aiming for the more lucrative orange groves of Florida. Planning further ahead, Roger had provisionally booked the bus from South America to Australia in a year's time.

The promotion work included having to take out all the tables so that a rock group, London Britches, could be photographed in the bus. The crew even drove around with them playing, which must have been a first. Bernice's diary recorded: 'I'm sat upstairs and the whole bus is vibrating from the group in our dining area. The tables are out and the room is choc-a-bloc with amplifiers, drums, guitars, cymbals and long-haired fellows. I walked downstairs and was amused to see the singer, complete with microphone, in our kitchen. They are very disorganised. I hope there's no noise abatement people here; I bet they haven't checked.

'Alec took seven us to supper and booze in his Rolls. The boys were goggle-eyes at his nanny all evening. He sounds so Bristol, it's as if he only arrived last week. He pranged the Rolls today, did $100 damage. Mike is uncertain whether to stay as his chauffeur until February, although he has been taking us around in it.'

Two days later, Bernice recorded that Mike had, indeed, decided to stay in Vancouver, while the bus moved on, until they found better jobs. Another one down!

On Tuesday, November 17, Bernice recorded: 'Daybreak start. Good to be on the road again. Scenery very bleak and roads very icy. Snow-capped mountains and then rocky, barren hills, like sand castles, with a few firs growing out of them. We passed meandering rivers with lots of fishermen, up to their thighs in the icy water. Must be mad. Have trouble with gears again, or could be the clutch. Was pitch dark at 4pm.'

Next morning Sally, always the first up, woke Don by mistake, and was told in no uncertain tones of her error. The journey was broken at Jasper, but once on the road again it started to snow heavily. The icy roads made progress slow, and they had to be careful over several unsafe-looking wooden bridges.

The following day they woke to find a further five inches of snow had fallen, the windows were iced up inside and out, and the bus was reluctant to start.

Once underway, the roads were surprisingly good, snow ploughs having been busy. The driver used a peephole cleared in the ice to see where he was going, as the windows stayed iced up all day.

Bernice recorded: 'We kept warm with constant coffee. The bus is creaking where everything is frozen. Fellow stopped us on the road, said he couldn't believe his eyes. He's been working in the mines for six months. Invited us to his home for showers. He was a little drunk and his wife was put out.

'She turned out to be very pleasant. He, however, became steadily drunker and nasty with it. Threw a beer can across the room and after most of us left had an argument with Don and Dave. Turns out he's French Canadian and hates the English.

'It's even colder, minus 29F. Curtains stuck to windows. Air freezing even with heads under blankets. Water tank frozen. Bus wouldn't start. Lit a fire under the engine to try and thaw it out…all it said was Pht! Got a parking ticket because we were stuck on the sidewalk.

'Had to get a truck out to recharge the batteries, and then had to be towed, which was quite scary on solid ice. The police let us off the ticket and arranged for us to have an escort, but as soon as we started the engine boiled over.

'We are now in a garage, so warm that the windows are running like waterfalls as they thaw out. The radiator has frozen and we can't even have a cup of tea because the pipes have also frozen. Jan has a match under the tap, but no success. We will have to keep the engine running all night to stop it freezing again. The boys put conditioner in to stop the diesel from gelling with the cold – this is why we have been getting air in the pump. Then the water pump went and the boys had to work in 12 below zero to fit a new one, with frequent cups of coffee laced with whisky. Waterfall of drips from ceiling as we lay in bed. Jan and Bob staying up all night to make sure the engine keeps running.

'Anyone who has never experienced snow in Canada will never understand the ferocity with which it can come down.

'It is like a huge blanket obliterating everything in sight, roads clear of snow become completely covered in seconds. Worst of all we knew we could not stop, because if we did our wheels would never be able to gain grip again, so we just had to keep going. Every day the weather got worse and our only hope was to get across Canada as quickly as possible.

'By the third day we had come down from the Rockies, away from the beauty of their towering peaks and endless snow-covered valleys, and on to the flat plains, mile after mile of snow-covered farmland.

'We had planned to travel mostly in summer. We could never have prepared for temperatures as low as minus 40F, which is what we experienced one night on the Prairies. We had to sleep in these terribly low temperatures with half an inch of ice formed from condensation on the inside of the widows.

'With little or no heating apart from the propane cooker in the kitchen life was very hard; we spent the days wrapped in blankets and the nights in our sleeping bags, dreaming of the Californian sunshine we had left behind. However, for all this it was an experience none of us would have missed. Every time we read about expeditions to the Poles and the terrible conditions endured we will remember our own Saskatchewan adventure.'

The crew were 'arrested' again – this time for not being able to see out of the window, as well as not having the correct permit. The bus had to go to a garage to thaw out. The town was Lloydminster, founded in 1903 by a wagon train of London and Scots families. One story was that they were so unaccustomed to the hard life there that they were taken advantage of, in so much as they were sold tin baths to stand in while they were cutting down trees so as not to cut their feet off!

A bolt fell out of the radiator as they started off, losing $15 worth of anti-freeze. Don fixed it in temperatures way below freezing.

Bernice wrote: 'We are on automatic pilot - a stick is propped between the steering wheel and the accelerator to keep us moving, so that the driver doesn't have to get his feet cold. Don has a blanket around his legs and a coat around his head as he drives. I watched a drip fall from the ceiling and stuck my finger out to touch it by which time it had frozen.'

On November 23, Bernice recorded that they had reached Winnipeg, Manitoba, amidst a landscape so flat that it took Roger half an hour driving at 40mph to reach a tower he had seen in the distance. The following day she wrote: 'Spent all day in bed, it's warmer.'

After travelling 412 miles in a single day, the weather was slightly warmer, so much so that they could see out of the windows for the first time for days.

Don saw some animals by the roadside that he thought might be cows or dogs, then realised they were black bears, and soon afterwards they saw the carcass of a skinned and gutted bear hanging up to dry. One night they parked at White River, noted as being the coldest place in Canada – a temperature of 72F degrees below was recorded there in 1936.

Bernice noted: 'It had taken us ten days to cross those snow-covered, windswept plains and on reaching the Province of Ontario, after having been able to see 30 or 40 miles ahead for so long, we found the smallest hills looked like mountains in the distance.'

The lakes were all covered in ice and it took the bus two and a half days to get around the northern coast of Lake Superior. The weather in Toronto seemed much warmer even though it was hardly above freezing.

'We felt triumphant in as much as we had beaten the Canadian winter. It was hard to believe that we had travelled right across the Continent – a distance of 3,000 miles – in such a short time in such terrible conditions," wrote Bernice.

The bus reached Sally's parents' farm on November 27 They had gone full circle, back to the area where the adventure had begun six months before. 'We all had hot baths,' Bernice wrote. 'It was quite nostalgic returning to our starting point, almost like having done a lap of honour.'

But no shortage of problems, She noted: 'I returned to the bus to find Bob chasing round, the wiring having shorted, tail lights on and smoke pouring from the windscreen wiper motor.'

They carried on without having solved the difficulty, leaving Sally behind for a month. She would work as a waitress at a country club and would catch up at Christmas.

CHAPTER 15

Back in Brookings I had run out of money, and wasn't seeing much of Mex because of her work commitments. It was boring and I felt beholden to Hippy Gene and John, who were happy to keep feeding me and providing money for me to go out and buy them (and me) beer.

One day we went golfing in one of the hearses, loaded with beer of course, which distracted us somewhat from the true spirit of the game.

On another occasion, Gene took me up into the hills at night poaching for deer. We had a powerful light that illuminated the creature's eyes from some distance, the idea being that we then shot it. I had one go with the surprisingly heavy rifle and was glad to say I missed it by some miles; I was probably more likely to endanger aircraft heading for San Francisco airport. The local Sheriff obviously heard the crack of the shot: we watched from our vantage point high up in the hills as he left town to look for us, and then we drove back home from the opposite direction.

At Niagara Falls, the crew enlisted the help of Norman Watson of the double-decker bus tours to solve the problem of the electrical shorting. His son worked alongside our mechanics at their garage (in the company of a racoon, an Alsatian dog, a llama and a deer) and soon worked out the problem: the wiring was earthed to the bus, so when it got wet it shorted. The dog and the racoon played well together, the dog biting at the racoon's backside when it was hanging above it, and the racoon then holding on with its front legs around the dog' s neck.

Jan fell down the trap-hole in the floor, which Don had left uncovered - both feet this time. Roger had been to Montreal to talk to Coca-Cola about sponsorship (another promising deal that never materialised) and Dave had a few days with his uncle in Oakville – with their return the bus would be back to seven members, a "full" crew in the absence of Sally, Mike and me!.

But en route to Toronto on the Queen Elizabeth Highway to pick up Roger, Don misjudged a bridge and there was a 'horrible crunching sound from upstairs. I expected to see a rip right through the centre of the roof,' wrote Bernice. However, it was not too bad, just a few more leaks.

Bernice visited an old customer on Yong Street, who was very pleased with the profit he had made from the brasses we sold him "first time round", but despite visiting many other shops she had little success in selling any more.

There was more word from some of the missing members. 'Seems Dave wants to find work in Oakville and join us in Florida, it's getting to be habit forming, and a letter from John tells us he is broke and hopes to reach us by Christmas,' Bernice's diary recorded. There was good news however: Mike expected to be back in a week. However Sally had decided to stay with her parents and rejoin the bus in Florida. Dave soon came back as well.

On Sunday, October 6, the bus left Oakville and crossed the border back into the USA at Lewiston Bridge. Obtaining a permit was now a well-worn route and Dave went to the Department of Highways in Buffallo and met the same people he had dealt with before. A permit was issued without a problem.

Dave and Don tried to get the bus started in icy conditions the following day. When they eventually started moving the police gave them an escort out of Rochester.

Bernice reported: 'I woke up next day and there was a 4-inch snowdrift at the side of the wardrobe. We went onto the roof and stuffed paper in a hole on the front lip, which must have been caused when we hit the last bridge. It snowed all day. Next day the 'likely lads' did it again, this time hitting a 12ft 6ins bridge. We reached Red Hook and Rex Maine took us out to dinner and bought us a lot of food.'

173

Two local friends said there was widespread corruption in the police force, with all the shops paying protection money and police turning a blind eye to gambling fraud. Jan and Dave did a radio show.

Roger put on an American accent to persuade the David Frost Show to book him for a TV spot in early January, and the crew met the American entertainer Jerry Desmond at the Oldstone Inn, publicity which pleased owner Stuart!

Mike was back, so now they were only one short. Me!

Back in Oregon I was growing increasingly disenchanted. I wrote home: 'The bus is nearing Toronto, Ontario, way over on the other side of the Continent and now I have to try and get over there. They left Vancouver before the month they gave me was up, which is a bit off.'

In retrospect, deciding to stay in Brookings had been a bad decision, my head turned by my new friends and the fact that I felt I needed a break from the bus. I only had myself to blame for my predicament.

Not only was I out of money, but I couldn't get any work. I went door to door along the main shopping street asking if they needed any jobs doing, but had no success at all. It was a small town and there was little employment. Without a car I had no way of getting to the coast or into the forests to find work.

Despite my plight, on finding a ten-dollar bill outside one of the shops I thought I ought to see if anyone inside had dropped it – they said 'No' but suggested I place it in the charity box! I did. What a fool!

In common with the rest of America the town was getting dressed for Christmas, with illuminated trees outside every house and extravagant decorations inside. My spirits were very unseasonal, however; I didn't know how I was going to find the money to get back to the bus.

The situation felt out of my control, which was a helplessness I had not felt before. My housemates cheered me up and for them I created and painted a "pub" sign – The Sewer Inn – and hung it from the front of the building. They were well impressed!

They then helped me paint the main room of the house as well. 'We painted one wall red, another green, another orange and another yellow and the ceiling dark blue. It looked awful,' I wrote home.

One pleasant interlude was a drive up to Eugene, 250 miles north, with Mex's boss to see if we could buy her a car. We did, a 1960 Volkswagen, $100 down and £44 a month.

'It was a real bargain,' I wrote home, 'I drove it back to Brookings next day and really enjoyed it. I stayed at a hotel overnight and met some nice people, chatted with a lawyer. Then for the next three days I stayed at the house, where Ermenia lives, and did some work for her boss; he paid me $3 and gave me all my meals. I feel better now than the last time I wrote, but I don't know what will happen. Maybe I will go back to the bus. I would like to work on a newspaper over here, the money is so good I could get a car and save enough for a house back in England in a couple of years.'

The bus crew visited New York on December 14. Bernice apparently didn't enjoy the visit. "We visited the Empire States Building, but couldn't get to the windows as it costs $1.60 to see the view, and a terrific draught comes up the lift shaft and nearly blows your head off," she said. It took them two hours by underground to get to Staten Island Ferry because "New York people are ignorant of routes, and they keep taking trains off."

They drove south in heavy snow and visited Washington on December 18. The Union Jack was flying from all the lamp posts alongside the Stars and Stripes, Nothing to do with the bus – Ted Heath, the UK Prime Minister, was on an official visit.

Bernice wrote: 'We got passes to the Capitol Building, but couldn't hear anything in the Senate because of poor loudspeakers, maybe that's why there were only a few senators present. Colesey tried his usual trick of dropping lighted matches in a paper bin. Jan hurried to the stream of smoke and took everything out. Then he and Bob were searched for being on a gallery where everyone who wasn't American had to have an ID and they didn't.'

The Lincoln memorial was "gigantic, impressive building,' she reported. 'When it's lit up at night it reflects in the very long oblong pool leading up to the long flight of steps...then a marble building with pillars round, in the centre of which is a statue of Lincoln looking out to the tall needle spire of Washington Memorial."

The crew had a guided tour of the White House.

At Arlington Cemetery, they were moved by the simplicity of John Kennedy's grave, and nearby the plain white cross that marked the last resting place of his brother Robert. At the grave of the Unknown Soldier, Bernice remarked: 'A very efficient guard was on duty, better than the one at Kennedy's graveside, who rushed off to get his cape when it started raining and when the guard changed the other fellow just walked up and chatted.

'They only had one pair of white gloves between them and had to pass them over."

At Newville a local man walked in and gave them a 4ft Christmas tree, which was much appreciated

On December 20, they left for the "other" Bristol – Bristol, Virginia – where they knew a warm welcome awaited them. Bernice wrote: 'They were all waiting for us, and had us tied up with religious activities, carol-singing tonight (four of us went with little children to an old people's home, absolute chaos, and the rest to lawyers' homes and the home of the Mayor to sing). It doesn't look like it will be a very boozy Christmas.'

They visited the Salvation Army and gave out toys to poor kids – 'Some parents were too shy or embarrassed to pick out something, and others not at all grateful. One said "why can't he have a bike too?"' reported Bernice. Mike made a good Santa, right build and a generous Ho, Ho, Ho.

Over the next few days they were guests of the YMCA and the Rotary Club (where they sang happy birthday to Joan) and Mayor Red Littleton wrote to the Lord Mayor of Bristol back home to say what a good job the crew were doing, how we had visited the jail and distributed gifts to the needy. A pharmaceutical company entertained them to Christmas dinner and gave them some of their products, cold pills and deodorants, nothing controversial!

Roger did a live TV discussion show and met the leader of an anti-Vietnam demo to be held in January – 'He wanted Roger to come so he could see how the National Guard intimidated students into fighting back,' wrote Bernice. 'We were so busy that we forgot we had been invited to tea at Mr and Mrs Heyes' home. We were an hour late. And then we were off to Dale McLaughlin's for another boozy party, the second booze up in this here Bible-belt, my my!'

On Christmas Eve there was, disappointingly, no mail from home.

The crew enjoyed a Christmas lunch as a local Lions group, and then an excellent turkey supper at Craig Rocket's house. 'It's fabulous, better than the White House,' wrote Bernice. Craig gave them a bottle of Bristol Cream sherry to toast the Queen and Roger made a punch of various bottles of booze collected on the way.

Christmas Day opened with a general reluctance to get out of bed, then an unwrapping of presents, the Royal toast, and a visit to the Martha Washington Restaurant, and old Colonial-style Inn, for an excellent meal. Bob and Jan went to a country club at the invitation of the Heyes. 'It is now very quiet in the bus,' wrote Bernice, 'eating our goodies and drinking the punch.

'Ted Littlleton arrived and we fed him the punch and frightened him to death telling him what was in it. It was a nice relaxing evening, and the boys played cards with the Mayor. We wondered what they were doing at home, and whether John was having a good time."

Not exactly! I was so broke back in Brookings that I rang my Mum and Dad up and asked if they could help, which they quickly did, sending money by Western Union. They were not well off, and they were very long suffering! In a letter home I said: 'Thanks very much for the £20 to everyone. I now have about 70 dollars in all and when I have another 70 I should be able to rejoin the bus. I really do appreciate it, when one has money in your pocket one has a bit of dignity as well.'

Christmas Day in Brookings was cold and snowy and lonely. John and Hippy Gene were with relatives so I was on my own. A few gifts from my Brookings friends couldn't cheer my up, so I decided to walk across town to where Mex lived and worked overlooking the river estuary. I knocked on the door and her boss opened it, pistol in hand! They hadn't been expecting any visitors. They were, however, most welcoming, and invited me to stay for the family Christmas dinner, which was very pleasant, before the cold walk home.

I had decided definitely to rejoin the bus. It was a good decision all round - soon after I left, Mex took up with Hippy Gene!.

I planned to travel by Greyhound bus to Virginia, but the bus crew very generously decided to find the money for me to fly, $169, and I did so on December 31, returning in time for New Year celebrations.

In a letter home I said: 'I took a Greyhound to Portland and then flew to Chicago, and then Cincinatti, and finally to Bristol Virginia in an old prop plane that was blown about in the turbulence. I had a terrible cold and could hardly speak.'

I was taken to the home of Fern and Pete Holmes, where Joan and Don had been staying, and went to bed after a shower because of my sore throat. However, I was fit enough to attend the New Year party the Holmes' hosted, for all the crew. I wrote in my diary: 'We had lots of booze and the Mayor wanted to play Nominated Whist all the time. We sang Auld Lang Syne at 12, and then everyone gradually passed out.'

Over the previous few days the crew had been working on the Mayor's farm, erecting fences. 'Mike and Bob have been doing it zig-zag fashion,' commented Bernice. They were also clearing trees and Joan was also doing some babysitting for the Ferns. The bus had been sitting idle for several days, but when it was switched on it started first time!

It snowed hard on January 1 and I was able to have a go at skiing, the first time for many years. It was good to be back on the bus, with all my friends, planning the next stage of the journey down to Florida, where we hoped to make enough money fruit picking to carry on to South America.

However, the good feeling I had at being back didn't last that long.

In a letter home on January 4 from near Atlanta, Georgia, I said: 'The atmosphere in the bus seems to have deteriorated with everyone moaning about Roger not telling anyone what plans he was making. Maybe it will improve later. Otherwise things look pretty bleak.'

By then, we were back on the road. We headed down route 11 towards Knoxville, encountering several low bridges, scraping one. We stopped to have a hard look at a bridge on the 411 at Englewood and a cop arrived and escorted us along the back roads and back to our route.

We parked for the night at Delano, near Athens, and were bothered by a couple, who wanted us to go to church.

Jan said we were just about to have a meal and when they insisted she added: "Anyway, we are not church-going people." They left a little annoyed.

As we moved into Georgia and passed through predominantly black areas, Roger and Bob were busy during overnight stops changing the engine oil and trying to get the headlights working.

Bernice discovered that $40 travellers' cheques had been lost and no numbers kept, which was annoying. We had swapped Monopoly for Nomination Whist to pass the time as we travelled, and Bernice and Joan decided to cook dinner, egg and chips, on the move, which horrified Mike, who was worried about the fire hazard.

We passed into Florida, soon noticing tropical vegetation appearing alongside the road, travelling 300 miles one day before we had to stop because of the lack of lights. The weather was noticeably a lot warmer.

We passed through Jacksonville and as we headed down the coastal Route 1 on Wednesday, January 6, with early drizzle turning to sunshine, a woman stopped us and asked if we wanted some oranges – we were in Orange County after all!

She and her husband, a watch maker, who showed us some clever card tricks, suggested we try local orange growers for work, and at the second attempt we succeeded. Mr C.H. Taylor of Mims (hereafter to be known as CH) said we could all have jobs from 7am on the following Monday.

As we moved on we could see across the Banana and Indian Rivers the huge structures of the Kennedy Space Station with a rocket on the launch pad, ready for the next Moon shot.

Almost at that moment we came down to earth with a bang, or rather a bang and a graunch, as the engine stopped. There was oil all over the engine and the road, and we lit flares to warn approaching traffic (they spluttered and went out).

Rog and Bob couldn't find anything obviously wrong apart from the fact that the oil cap had blown off, and after enlisting the help of a friendly motorist to fetch some more oil, we carried on.

Two friendly cops said they thought we were travelling evangelists. Holy cow! Whatever next!

The following day as we headed for Miami the engine stopped twice more and Rog diagnosed a floating piston (whatever that is). We also had no water in the radiator. Although uncertain of the height of the overpasses we decided to take the Freeway and as luck had it they were all over 15ft and we made Miami by 4pm.

An attractive girl from the Consul, Margaret, guided us to Palm Island, a rather exclusive residential area, where she lived, and after initial opposition from the owner, who called our bus a "truck," we were allowed to park in a vacant lot, not 200 yards from where Al Capone once lived.

We were told that everyone who has lived there since has dug the whole garden up looking for buried loot. My diary recorded: 'Went on Tom Adams Show (TV). We have been promised a sealed beam unit (for the front headlight). Saw sign which said Beware of falling coconuts.'

Our mixed lifestyle continued next day. I went to Immigration and picked up a new entry permit extension (they hadn't twigged on that we had been working), Rog, Bern and Mike went to see Ervin Kimble, MD of Contrall Packaging (potential advertiser) and I was then interviewed by a reporter Bee Hines (behinds!). The rest of the gang had gone to look for that sealed beam unit, but they couldn't find one that fitted. Rog phoned Sally (still in Canada with her relatives) and she said she would be back soon.

Apparently there were mixed feelings about us among island residents; someone complained about us to the police, but Nat Ratner, vice-President of the Landowners Association, said it was good to have us there to liven things up a bit and invited us to a party. With the temperature in the 70s, we did some fishing and had a great time.

Next day, the Sunday, we headed back to Mims, reaching it about 10.30am and were directed down dusty side roads to a parking spot next to a bar, within sight of the sea and quite near the railway line to Cape Kennedy space station. We plugged our electrics into the bar's supply.

I recorded: 'The bar was quite busy – an attractive girl who looked about 19, but was, in fact, 14, beat me at pool, and then Dave beat some American chap and won a beer! Dave and I went out for the evening to a bar in Titusville with a chap named Dan, who said he was an officer of the Klan and stood to attention when they played Yankee Doodle Dandy as if it was the Klan song!

There was a lot of anti-black sentiment, which we tried to ignore. He said he would like to take me to a Klan meeting (months later I would interview the head of the Klan for Today newspaper, mock him for his attitude and spend a sleepless night worrying that his thugs would break in and get me!). Dan was very drunk when he drove us home. We were woken three times in the night by trains as we were parked only about 10 yards from the track!

CHAPTER 16

We started work for CH the following day, a Monday, $3.50 a bin, slow, hard work carrying ladders and climbing up into trees. CH told us we could park at his home, plug into his electrics and use the toilet and shower in his garage. We could also get cheap diesel from him.

A lot of black workers were arriving, some from the Bahamas, but the way it was arranged was for us to work separately from them, as a team. They lived away from the farmhouse in a squalid collection of huts.

My diary recorded: 'We are going to try a system where someone different gets up first every morning and makes tea and breakfast for all. And we will work five days for the bus, one for ourselves and have the Sunday off. There is some question about whether we should have social security numbers, but CH said not to bother.'

The following day we did 17 boxes or oranges, three more than the first day. 'We found it easier on the big trees to drop the oranges for someone else to pick them up,' I recorded. Bruised fruit? No bother!

We carried on picking oranges and grapefruit until Friday, the low point being when Bernice injured her back, the high point being taken to Cocoa Beach by CH's daughter, Tricia, where we sat in on a lecture at her college before relaxing on the beach.

We had arranged a visit to the Space Station, and the press were there to take photos of the bus next to full-scale replicas of the lunar landing craft and a Saturn V engine. All great fun, apart from visiting Complex 34, where astronauts Grissom, White and Chaffie had been killed in a fire during a simulated take-off.

Dave's diary recorded: 'We went to the Visitor Centre where we parked the bus alongside space rockets and the Lunar Landing Module mock-up.

'The press were there and took a lot of photos and interviewed us. The management gave us a guide and off we went in our bus. The highlight was of the tour was being able to park at the viewing area for the Apollo 14 Moon mission due to blast off on 31 January 1971. The rocket stands 363' tall.'

On the Saturdays we worked for ourselves earning eight dollars each. It's amazing how eight dollars can cheer you up. For me it meant I could buy some baccy. Several of us smoked pipes as it was cheaper than cigarettes and as previously mentioned you could mix up your own ingredients with straight baccy.

You could smoke anywhere in those days – no restrictions in bars or shops. Back in England, however, smoking had been banned on the Isle of Wight railways, those former London Underground trains which rattled and rolled between Ryde and Shanklin.

My brother, Tony, told me one fellow traveller was so incensed at being barred from smoking his pipe that when the doors slid closed at the start of the journey he stuck his pipe between them, puffing away on the stem inside with the smoke bellowing forth from the bowl outside.

The joke was on him, however, because when the train reached Ryde Pierhead they all disembarked from the doors on the other side, leaving the smoker desperately trying to pull his pipe through doors that remained tight shut!

We had heard from Sally at last - still in Canada having trouble getting her visa renewed, but hopefully now on her way. Apparently she fell foul of a customs officer, who said she did not have enough money on her to enter the USA, and refused to believe she was part of a bus crew travelling the world. She went home and her dad's boss, Mr Smith, pulled some strings so she could cross the border.

She arrived on the Sunday when all of us except Don and Dave, who were picking oranges for pocket money again, had gone to the beach with Tricia. Sally joined us (bringing 30 dollars for our funds) for a visit to the cinema to see Catch 22, the tickets cadged by Tricia, who had become very friendly.

I was busy cabling a story and photos to the Daily Express, because there was a postal strike back home, and I also spoke to a chap, who ran the Piccadilly Club in Orlando, who was interested in us doing a promotion for him.

It became a tiresome day: 'Snotty Mrs Barclay at the British Consul was rude again, this time because she had to pay $1.50 on a parcel for us,' my diary recorded. 'It has been a difficult day in the trees, which are very big with small fruit. We made about $66. And it is very cold, near freezing tonight.'

It was painful working with cold hands the following day and huge thorns on some of trees ripped into our clothes and skin. Sally was on hand to tend to our wounds. Florence Nightingale!

We made just $55 all day. Next day we did better - $108 working on Temple oranges at $4 a bin.

Sally recalls: 'After working in the orange groves, Bernice and I were given 10 dollars to replace our working clothes from the kitty.

'Other than that we had each made one dress that was suitable to wear to the embassies, etc, and had one pair of smarter sandals rather than flip flops.'

It was an odd set up for us English visitors to understand; the blacks were seasonal workers from the Bahamas, and were treated very differently from us.

Whereas we lived in CH's backyard, literally, they lived in wooden shacks some distance away, and were not encouraged to visit CH at home, nor fraternise with us (and we were discouraged from talking to them).

We received a letter from the British Consul, saying they were angry with us for using them as an office. Roger phoned them up straight away and complained that they, in turn, were not sending on our mail and had in fact opened one urgent letter without sending it on.

We also had CH complaining that we used the pick-up too much, and were only to use it going to work and travelling within Titusville

Heavy rain disrupted work, and, as I recorded: 'Mike had his usual early morning battle with his ladder to see who would be boss, and as usual the ladder won!'

We had the occasional illness or torn muscle. My diary recorded: 'Sunday – Dave hurt his back and Ripper fell into a tree and felt funny.'

But apart from bruises and scratches, we were all in pretty good shape because of the hard physical work we were doing, and on a sensible low-fat, low alcohol diet (well done, Mike the chef!). It was a good job we didn't have anyone regularly ill because as I noted: 'Several people not in favour of sharing the Saturday money with those who are ill.'

The next week we had nine working, though Jan had foot trouble and Rog a bad knee.

I returned late from a date back in the orange grove - a walk under the stars seems unlikely - and couldn't get into the bus because the door had jammed, so I slept in an old car.

We were not making a lot of money, however, less than 50 dollars a day, and I noted: 'Spending too much money on food. We have to cut down to one egg in the morning and other things.'

On Saturday, January 30, 1971, crowds were gathering all along the coast to await the launch of Apollo 14, the third rocket to the Moon from Cape Kennedy. Our boss said the best view of the launch would be from the top of an orange tree, but he probably had an ulterior motive. On the Sunday we drove the bus into Titusville. It was a cloudy day and the roads were packed. Our bus caused a great deal of interest – "Is it one bus put on top of another?" asked one passer-by.

We attempted to drive along the coast road to get as close to the launch site as possible, but were forced to turn back because the bus couldn't get past overhanging trees.

I recorded: 'We drove on to the One again and up to the Shipwreck Bar. There were people everywhere, but there was a place next to the bar, between cars and campers, where we could park. So we did.

'There are friendly people all around, particularly a camper load of fellows from Tennessee, who had a black chauffeur, called Smith.

'They gave us beer and we talked a lot and they cooked us some sausage. Rain came down with about 10 minutes to go, sending all the spectators scurrying for cover. At 8.2 minutes to go, the count was held. When the rain cleared, the count was resumed.

Forty minutes late, a bright glow appeared under the rocket, stayed there for a long moment and then it slowly rose into the air as everyone frantically took photos.

'It had gone into cloud within ten seconds. No noise whatsoever. But very worthwhile for the people who had come so far.'

Dave wrote: 'Apollo 14 lifted off at 16.03hrs. It was a spectacular sight with lots of smoke and flame before she began to lift off the pad and built up speed to get off the ground. Watching her ascend into a blue sky knowing there were people on board was quite awesome and I think this is one of the events in life that stays with you forever.

'The actual launch was comparable with the launches I had seen when firing the Corporal missile in the Army, but this definitely had the edge.'

For the record, Commander Alan Shepard, Command Module Pilot Stuart Roosa, and Lunar Module Pilot Edgar Mitchell launched on their nine-day mission on January 31, 1971 at 4:04:02 pm local time after a 4- minute, 2-second delay due to launch site weather restrictions, the first such delay in the Apollo programme. Shepard and Mitchell made their lunar landing on February 5. Shepard, Roosa, and Mitchell landed safely back in the Pacific Ocean on February 9.

We got home safely to Mims, too.

Far from the technology that took Man to the Moon, the continuing mail strike was holding up delivery of a new axle for the bus. It was stuck in Baltimore, awaiting the correct paperwork, and we were liable for customs storage charges.

Money was a problem with so many mouths to feed; some weeks we made over $1,000, others half that.

I had also been unable to send my parents an anniversary card. In a letter home I said: 'I suppose Dad is not working, what a bind

(Dad worked at Lake Post Office). Still, they are very badly paid. Over here the postmen have little square mail vans with the driving seat on the pavement side, so they can put the mail in the little mail boxes without getting out of the van!"

CHAPTER 17

On Friday, Feb 5 Roger suddenly announced he was leaving the bus. He was returning to England to study at Oxford University. It was a huge shock to us (and his wife, Bernice) and a massive blow to our plans to travel around the world.

There was no doubt Rog and Bernice had always been the driving force behind the project, and as our leader he had been able, through force of personality, to keep us working together when at times different factions had been pulling us apart. It was a small taste, perhaps, of what he might expect a great deal many years later as a top health union official and in negotiating a deal between religious extremists in Northern Ireland as Chair of the Parades Commission.

Bernice said she would stay with the bus at least until South America.

She wrote later: 'Before leaving England Roger had been in the Docks Police - he was too short for the 'proper' police. I was working as a secretary for the Regional Hospital Board. He had been doing a correspondence course on trade unionism and unbeknown to me had been offered a place at Ruskin University.

'This only came to light nine months into the trip when Roger decided to leave the bus and continue his studies. At this time I was really upset, not least, as I thought that as the leader he was leaving the team in the lurch, to put it politely. Everyone was understanding and offered their good wishes when he left. I was determined to stay to see it through."

Dave saw it this way: 'For some time Roger and Bernice have been in intense discussion and there has been some tension in the air. We had a meeting today and Roger dropped the bombshell announcement that he is to leave the bus. He has been given the chance to go to Oxford University to study with the eventual aim of going into politics.

'He intends to leave the bus soon and probably before the end of the month. Bernice is planning to stay on board as she wants to continue the adventure into Central and South America and then review her decision. All of this has caused a lot of feeling amongst the crew and everything is very uncertain. It may cause a lot of problems. We will need to decide on a new leader."

The loss of Roger, as the leader and as a companion, was a turning point. He was the driving force. When there were disagreements, Roger was always ready to listen to all sides, but beneath the banter and good humour that sometimes won people over he exercised good sense and a firm resolve.

We didn't waste much time in selecting a leader. On Monday 8 February, Dave wrote in his dairy: 'Rain, more rain and high winds. We were not able to work. We held a crew meeting and John has been elected leader with immediate effect. There was discussion on what to do when/if someone else leaves. The main issue is what they can take with them financially. They would have worked and input to the kitty, but could they take so much it affects the rest? The main conclusion was to re-register the company in everyone's' name and to have a written agreement between ourselves that should anyone leave then they forfeit all."

We decided to give Roger $200 for his flight home. He had wanted to work alone in the orange groves to make the money, but we decided it would not be practical.

My diary that dismal day recorded some good news: 'Mike bought a 64-dollar short wave radio for $50. Now we can hear the soccer results!'

In a letter home, I said: 'I didn't really want the job, I prefer to help behind the scenes. There are a lot of responsibilities in this, lots of decisions to make, and always impossible to please everyone. The bus goes in my name, so if we get around the world OK, I shall be famous in Bristol! They all think it is a bit amusing, an Isle of Wight person leading a Bristol crew!"

Life went on. It was Jan's birthday the next day, so Bob took her breakfast in bed, and then made everyone else in bed a cup of tea. Sally and I weren't there, we were out partying! On one occasion, the group's social life was not so pleasant. We went into a local tavern where there was a band and the bandleader commented "We are having a barbecue soon, nothing better than barbecued n......" The audience thought it highly amusing. Racism was rife.

It didn't take long for trouble to start on the bus. I recorded: 'I had some trouble with Dave yesterday. They all seem to want to make decisions together, as a group, but that is ridiculous when it goes so far as having to call a vote on whether to stop at the post office, or when to have a tea break. Things like that should be left to me to decide. Anyway, now I am insisting that the group should decide by majority vote on everything, no matter how small, and see if they realise how daft it is.'

We carried on picking oranges. We had to. We needed money to carry on the trip. But it was not easy pickings.

On one day Dave recorded: 'Awkward trees and smelly ditches. What a combination.' And on another: 'I was unable to work today. My back is very painful and I can only take short steps. The rest had a very disappointing day and CH has warned we could be laid off for a few days.'

Life had its ups and downs. I was standing on top of my ladder, picking oranges, when suddenly it lifted three foot in the air. I shouted out and Sally said: "Oh, sorry. I thought it was heavy!"

On another occasion, Sally was standing in a tree while I moved her ladder for her, and the branch broke. Sally plunged over 15 feet to the ground, which knocked the wind out of her and left a deep imprint of her body in the soft earth. Luckily, she was unhurt.

In between the hard work in the orange groves, we had other duties.

194

Jan wrote to cigarette firms to try to tempt them into advertising on the side of the bus. We considered sending Bob and Jan to the Miami Boat Show to see if they could get a cheap winch and more ads, and pick up the new differential at the same time, but because of the postal strike it still had not been processed.

We briefly considered finding another person to join us, another pair of hands, but decided against it. Bob, Don and Dave were to look into the possibility of getting a winch, front bumper and cow-catcher and a sump cover.

One day we chased a racoon and when it climbed a tree a fusillade of oranges failed to dislodge it. We had good days – "small trees and big fruit, $131" - and bad days – "back to earth with a bump, $76 on big trees."

Our good friend, Rex Maine, took some of the lads out for the evening to a couple of bars. And then he presented us with an air conditioning unit.

On Monday, February 22, Rex took Roger to New York for his flight home. It was my birthday. Bernice cooked me a bread pudding. It went down very well. She must have been upset, but carried on as usual. I don't think we knew then how Roger's departure would affect us. It was a fatal blow to the trip.

Bob and Jan arrived back from the boat show with disappointing news – no-one was interested in using us for advertising or promotions. But they had sorted out a deal where a firm would print 6,000 postcards of us for £100 dollars, to be sold to the public and used for promotions. Sally and I sold a brass hunting horn to the Fox Inn for $11 and they said they wanted a stuffed fox as well. First, find one!

Dave recorded: 'Five of us, Sally, Joan, Don, John and self at work. Did 14 bins. Roger left to return to England. Mike starts work tomorrow. Bob and Jan due back tonight. Rex has bought us an air conditioner unit. $139!!! What a bloke.

'Cleared out all the stores from under the seats into the garage ready to start sorting out. Had a short meeting. Night school to learn Spanish starts tomorrow."

Mike was finding it difficult working amongst the big trees, but he managed to get a few days gardening, and the offer of more hours in a nursery at Titusville if he can get there.

We were seeking advice on crossing South America, particularly from motoring organisations – 'It appears there might be a northern route to the Amazon,' I wrote.

Dave's diary recorded: 'Friday, March 5th 1971 - Another bad day. Moved groves and CH reckoned it would be good picking at $4.50 a box but we only managed $67.Cheque for last week was $619 which was good. Mike has spent a couple of days gardening. Everyone is calling him Percy Thrower.

'Saturday, March 6th 1971 - Pickers complained about the fruit. Price upped to $5 a box and we made a hundred dollars. Kitty stands at just over $4,000 now. Went out in evening for a few beers.'

We visited a woman called Mrs Ridenour, who read our fortune in cards and from our palms. She suggested that we were all running away from something, rather than looking for something. Bob was very loving, Sally liked to be independent, Mike was a married type, Bernice was scared, Jan insecure, and I was not easily influenced. I believed every word of it!

Mike started work at the nursery at $1.15 an hour thanks to a NASA photographer, Red Williams, who had fixed up transport for him. He would later take our photograph for the postcards, another example of the wonderful support we received from the many friends we made across the States. They were most generous and hospitable.

Dave's diary recorded: 'Thursday, March 25th 1971. Same as usual. Poor picking only $70. Did a beautiful dive out of a tree today. About 18ft up when the branches parted and I slid sideways on my ladder out the tree. Fended off a palm tree and as the ladder hit the ground I stood up and stepped off. Jan had watched and was amazed. I thought it a pretty good effort as well and, though a little shaken, carried on picking.

'Friday, March 26th 1971 - Finished the grove at last. Just in time as it started to rain as we finished the last tree. Kitty now stands at $5,400.

'Monday, March 29th 1971 - Picking grapefruit and the trees got bigger. Had a meeting in the evening. Decided to leave here on June 10th. If we can clear $500 a week we shall leave with over $10,000.'

I was suffering from boils on the back, caused by infected scratches from the trees and dust in the eyes. Sally arranged a visit to a doctor and put drops in my eyes. She had given me a pack of beer for my birthday and treated me to an evening out. Sally and I were always ready to go out for the evening, mostly separately, and I wrote home: 'I have managed to get the lads out for a drink. They are terrible. None of them ever come out, just Sally and I, though I hasten to add not together! The rest just sit in after work and watch TV or go to bed. They are getting very much in a rut here.'

The differential arrived. Bob and Dave fitted it. 'It was far easier than we expected though we had our problems. We used the facilities of the Mims. C.G.A. work-shop which was very useful,' Dave recorded.

Don and I used fibreglass to repair some of the holes in the roof caused by collisions with bridges and trees, and Bob started on the installation of the air conditioner. Dave fixed the rear lights. We had a row with CH as he didn't like some of us drinking with coloured workers in the driveway.

Dave was making friends through his Spanish classes.

On Saturday, April 10, he recorded: 'Went out to Susie's house in the evening. Had a great time with all her friends. Charlie has fixed our cow catcher on now."

And then, on Tuesday, April 13th 1971 – 'Picking still poor, but with Mike's money we should pull up for the week. Went out in evening to the house of one of the girls, Margie, that we met last Saturday. Lot of people there for a Bible study session. Very interesting.'

On Monday, April 19th he dropped a bombshell. He later reported: 'Had a meeting and told everyone that I am considering leaving after South America. Harvey and Becky, two of the Bible Study class, came round in the evening and stayed for a while. Harvey is an expert parachutist and has invited some of us out next Sunday to the airfield."

Dave was obviously as unsettled as I was. I couldn't say at the time, but I was thinking seriously about how long I would stay with the bus. Like Dave, I had made friends in the community, and found them a welcome change after so many months living in such close quarters to so many people.

On Saturday, April 24th 1971, Dave's diary recorded: 'Went with Don to do some painting. It rained. In evening went to hear Nicky Cruz, an ex-gangster turned preacher, give a talk on his life at the Baptist Church. After had coffee with Nancy Bennett.'

Later, he added: 'I have been attending a Bible study group on Tuesday evenings. It has given me great help in my personal life and renewed by faith. Several people were very helpful in this. Mike Furslow and his fiancée, Margie Murphy, talked with me a great deal and have become good friends of mine. They have always been willing to run me around to meetings and to take me out. They are all really tremendous people. On the weekend of May 7th – 9th I went to a retreat at Lake Yale near Orlando. A great experience.'

On May 9th we had been away for one year.

I do remember that Dave found great comfort from his Bible studies group, and he gathered us together to explain how he felt about us. It was hard for him, and we admired him for it.

Maybe I should have done the same.

On May 10 I left the bus, quietly, telling only Mike. It had been building up for some time. In a letter home on April 19, I said I had arranged an interview on a local newspaper, and I added that I had written two children's stories. I had finally finished the one about a big red school bus, and sent them both off to magazines. Sadly, they were rejected.

In a letter on April 28, I went further: 'I desperately want to get out of the rest of the trip for a variety of reasons. I am fed up with living at such close quarters; I loathe having no money with which to buy myself a stamp or a beer; the trip is going to take much longer than I first thought, three years probably and I feel I ought to be earning money for the future.'

If I had learned the lesson of Oregon, I would not have left the bus. But I had had enough; I didn't need the group any more and felt they could get along fine without me. I have never regretted that decision.

I didn't have a job to go to, but I felt something would turn up. Again, the confidence of youth! Reassuringly, I felt closer to home on the Atlantic side of the US, even though there was 4,000 miles of ocean between us.

I had regularly been seeing local women and although one relationship in particular was still enjoyable, it had thrown up another issue. 'I never have the money to take friends to a bar or a dance or buy them petrol,' I said in my letter home. 'Sometimes the girl I am with pays for my lunch or buys me cigars, and this has happened before.

'It happened in Oregon, where the lads used to pay for me to eat and drink, and in San Diego where Chris did the same, and often when other people treat us all to food or give us clothes or beer, and it will happen again, and I am determined it will not happen any more because I won't remain in such a position to make it necessary. One doesn't realise what it is to lose one's pride and dignity.'

Reading that now it seems pompous, but it was heart-felt.

I can't remember where I stayed the day I left but in a letter home I said: 'I have a job and an apartment lined up in Titusville. It's in a big block of apartments and costs $16 (£6.50) a week and though there is little furniture in it I am sure it will be OK.'

My latest relationship had ended almost as soon as it started (she was engaged when I met her). Very impulsive, these American women! I was not thinking long-term and she wanted someone reliable, and had a child to think of. Reliable I wasn't! She had also lost her job as a dental assistant and was planning to move north to find one.

CHAPTER 18

I went to live in a house full of recovering drug addicts, the Palm Hotel and Apartments at Titusville, thanks to the generosity of the owner (he let the addicts live there pretty well free) who asked me just to paint the outside of house as payment for my lodgings (I was pretty good at climbing ladders after months in the orange groves). I didn't touch hard drugs, just the odd funny fag, or cannabis in my pipe, but I got on well with this crazy bunch, particularly after a few weeks when I bought a black light and painted vines across all my bedroom walls in luminous paint. It freaked them out!

The other residents seemed to respect the fact that I was a few years older than most of them and they didn't invade my space unless I wanted them to. There was one incident when a girl tapped on the skylight in my room in the middle of the night. I let her in. We chatted a bit and then a bit more. For those who remember it was a bit like the film Brief Encounter 'with brass knobs on,' as we kids used to say. Then she left and 'we went our separate ways.'

I also found a job working as a feature writer on Today newspaper at Titusville. It didn't come easily. I wrote to the editor and he replied that he didn't have any vacancies. So I cadged a lift 20 miles to the newspaper office, walked in a back door, found my way to his office and just walked in. I pretended not to have had his letter. He was decent enough to suggest I write some features for him.

One article, I remember, was about a narcotic agent with the best convictions record in the state. I didn't take him home with me!

The editor was impressed and it was arranged that until I could get a work permit I would be paid about £60 a week! Riches! I was able to pay my landlord the £6.50 a week for my apartment.

He was a well-respected local architect with a great sense of social responsibility, so much so that he allowed drug addicts, ex-offenders and the disabled to live cheaply in the apartments.

I wrote home: 'He calls me 'our little bit of culture.' I get on well with them all, though I don't get involved with any of them. Three were arrested for heroin possession yesterday.'

More worries for my Mum!

It was great to be a free agent again. After a few weeks I moved into an apartment at Cocoa Beach with a Lebanese guy, Sam, who was even more mad about girls than I was, bought a car for 1,000 dollars, and passed a Florida driving test.

I enjoyed my work at Today newspaper, working on Sunrise magazine, travelling across the State to interview, among others, the world's fattest man, the owner of the Heartbreak Hotel ("the locals were heartbroken because I got it" he said) and covering the opening of Disneyworld, which was champagne-fuelled, spectacular and quite wonderful.

I drove there in my car, became quite drunk, phoned in my copy (which was really rather good), tried to chat to Boston Pops conductor Arthur Fiedle, who had waved his baton over 140 musicians representing some of the world's major symphony orchestras, which was embarrassing for both of us, and then went back to my car via the monorail system, playing footsie with the woman, who was sitting opposite (with her husband). Oddly, they invited me back to their place but I declined - a rare moment of common sense. I was not so sensible that, still drunk, I drove home.

I had an unpleasant interview with the Florida Grand Dragon of the Klu Klux Klan at a Klan meeting. The Klan had become marginalised, and was a bit of a joke, but the Klansmen were very intimidating, packing numerous handguns and shotguns in the cabins of their pick-up trucks.

I wrote a scathing piece about the meeting, and the day it was published I lay awake all night waiting for them to seek retribution!

I interviewed a Playboy Bunny on Cocoa Beach and she frolicked in the surf with her dog, Poo Poo, for Greg Leary, our photographer. "Why do you all him Poo Poo?" I asked. "Because he's a little shit," she said.

Frog gigging made an interesting feature - you glide at speed across the Everglades on an air boat, similar to a hovercraft, and when your floodlight picks out the flash of a frog's eyes you stab it with a long-handled fork, hoping you haven't made a mistake and stabbed an alligator. I did not enjoy the frog legs - they were a bit like tough chicken wings. I also interviewed several air hostesses about their night life when off-duty. That was my own idea…

You can't work at Titusville and not cover rocket launches from Cape Canaveral. I interviewed the chap in charge of deciding whether the weather was OK for the launch, and then stood with thousands on the beach or breakwaters (we all had to get out along the rough rock jetties protruding into the sea as far as we could go for the best vantage point) waiting for him to give the all clear so the launch could proceed.

I travelled from my air-conditioned apartment to my air-conditioned office in my air-conditioned car. It was hot outside, but mostly you stayed in! I had a good friend in photographer Greg, who specialised in unusual techniques, and once made me kiss a delightful girl for half an hour so he could take a photo of a light shining through our lips. I could have gone on longer. I smoked lots of pot, drank lots of beer and went out with several girls.

I decided to travel back to England before Christmas 1971, I was ready to go home for good, even though my editor attempted to get me a permit to live and work in the States permanently.

You can't go on enjoying life as a travelling bachelor for ever, can you? Can you? Maybe it suits some. But I needed roots, and I wanted to see my family.

I came back to the Isle of Wight (my Mum and Dad were relieved and delighted to see me) and heard shortly afterwards that the permit to stay in the US had been refused. I was glad. I wrote to Sam and asked him to sell my car and guitar (which I had never learnt to play).

I returned to the good old Isle of Wight County Press, and was given the job of covering the rural West Wight, which was so quiet that I sometimes did the 9am police/ambulance calls from my bed!

CHAPTER 19

But let's get back to the bus, the hero of our story. When I left, they converted my bunk into storage space. They were preparing for the next stage of the journey, into Central America.

Dave's diary read: 'Monday, May 31st 1971 Usual picking. Meeting in evening. Got rather stormy at one point and Bernice blew up and said she was going home. Oh well!!

'Tuesday, June 1st, 1971: Day off from picking. Doctor's instead. Two jabs. Typhus and Typhoid one in each arm. Wandered around town after before going over to Jim's. Bernice staying.'

Don remembered one incident, whilst driving CH's brand new pick-up truck. He found a pistol in the dashboard, and brandished it when he and Bob got out to start work in the trees. "It was stupid really, but we were playing cowboys and somehow I pulled the trigger and said 'Stick em up' and the thing went off, luckily missing Bob. Joan was really mad with me, and said how stupid I had been. She was really fond of Bob, mothered him I suppose."

More serious trouble was brewing. One of our girls fell out with one of the female pickers, over one of the black male pickers, and the black girl threatened to shoot her. How that happened is beyond imagination, and probably best not to go there, but it should never have occurred at a time when all of us were aware that racial intolerance was widespread in the USA.

The boss was worried – he started wearing a gun and told the group that our girl would have to leave. They had to go down with CH to the shacks where the black workers lived and get our girl out. The Sheriff's department were called and it was finally agreed that our girl would leave the area, staying with a friend in Alabama, before rejoining the bus later. Only on that basis were the group allowed to continue working.

With the day of the group's departure imminent, Dave found himself guest of honour at his church, and was presented with several gifts.

He recorded: 'It really knocked me for six that people cared so much. The bus held a tea party in the afternoon for all our friends to say a farewell before leaving. John did a big story on us which appeared in the Sunrise magazine."

On Thursday, June 10th 1971, the eight remaining members of the group cleared up the site, said farewell to the Taylors and travelled 80 miles to St Augustine before parking up for the night. They were heading back to Mexico City, via Texas, and then on across Central America to Colombia.

Central America was an unstable area, beset by poverty and war. Nicaragua, in particular, was under the oppression of a dictator, who amassed great amounts of wealth despite the plight of the people. Efforts by guerrilla groups to overthrow the Government would end in a horrific war which did not end until 1987.

On Monday, June 28th the bus was parked in Mexico City. There were technical problems, and disagreements.

Dave's diary recorded: 'Late start. Lots of wandering around with nobody making any moves. Angry words all round. Moved to Cummins where we arrived at 1.30p.m. Whilst waiting for mechanics to finish lunch Don said that he and Joan were leaving if things didn't improve. This is going to be discussed later. Bus still on jacks with a spring half on at end of work, so had to leave it.'

A new spring was fitted, but when the bus was lowered it bent. Dave went to see a specialist firm about it, but they said that new stronger springs or the present ones with extra leaves and re-tensioned would have to be fitted. This would raise the bus height about 6".

News from Guatemala said that there were three bridges on the proposed route with a maximum height of 14' 1". Discussions took place on whether to lower the bus roof took place, but no decision was taken because Sally and Bernice were staying at a pub.

Sally's diary recorded: 'New springs on the back put bus up six inches in height. Discussed chopping 10 to 12 inches off top of bus, but idea was rejected. Hope springs will stand the strain.'

The exhaust was re-built and re-fitted and work started on replacing the cow catcher. Fancy that - a bus with a cow catcher!

The following day Dave didn't feel too good, so stayed in bed most of the day. His spirits improved when the group went to the Piccadilly Pub at 6:15p.m. Carmen Allamilla, the girl who proposed last year, was there. 'A great reunion but she's still proposing!' Dave recorded.

Dave recalls: 'Near Mexico City is the ancient Aztec city of Teotihuacan. We took a day trip with the bus to see it. The Temples of the Sun and moon were terrific. We climbed to the top of the Sun Pyramid and met a chap from Gloucester."

And so the journey progressed, down to Guatemala, bringing down more overhead wires, Indians waving, customs officers checking the crew at gunpoint.

As people looked in at us in our goldfish bowl, we looked back - they were getting on with life as we all do, although of different cultures.

For some discrimination made it all the more difficult, whether racial, religious, sexual or simply male domination.

In many countries the extended family is very important and they stay much closer, far more than in the UK, where family members often move away to live and work.

This family closeness is particularly important in poorer countries, where it helps them to get through hard times, and is very noticeable in the way they care for their aged.

Of course, extremes of poverty and wealth are evident everywhere, including the UK, where the wealthy seem to get richer all the time.

At times, the generosity of poor people took our breath away.

Mike wrote: 'We were always on the receiving end of gifts, whether it was food or equipment, so it was rewarding to return the favour: here's one story that may illustrate that.

'One late afternoon in Guatemala we pulled in alongside a building with a high wall surrounding it. It was a clinic staffed by nursing nuns and sisters. I approached a figure who appeared through a gate and asked in my halting Spanish if we could park safely for the night.

A big smile encased her face as she replied "It's OK! I realised you were English by your calling card." She nodded towards the bus. "How can we help?"

'She was an Irish nun. We were invited in and introduced to her companions. Just then a bell rang and an obviously very poor lady with a small baby appeared asking for help. The baby had a severe rash and had flies pestering her. One of the sisters immediately took the baby away to treat her.

'Sally asked how they received medical supplies and apparently they raised money from the local community to buy them.

'I asked if there was any way we could help, as we had several large boxes of Complan, a food additive, with which to help people to recover after illnesses. We asked if we could give them some? There were nods of approval all around from the crew and off Sally and I went to get them. We came back with a large black bag full and the Sisters' eyes were mirrored in astonishment at how much there was.

'They invited us to have a freshly-made lemonade – delicious - and we moved out onto the patio, where there was a huge musical instrument. I thought it was a xylophone, but our host explained it was a marimba and asked if we would like to hear it played.

'The evening melted away with the soft sound of the marimba played in total harmony by three local people at a time in pure white cheesecloth shirts and trousers, the temperature in the low 70s, with the moon rising between the mountains. The palm trees surrounding us rustling gently in the soft breeze.

'It was a never-to-be-forgotten moment to be able to give something back to the Sisters of this clinic and the local population. Farewells were said and I know I went to sleep that night at peace with the world.'

On Monday, July 5th 1971 they travelled from Acatlan to Oaxaca, an old Colonial town. They held a meeting in evening. Mike, after much beating around the bush, was elected leader. Jan and Bob threatened to leave as a result.

Sally recorded on July 8: 'Don (driving) got lost in town looking for a market, and couldn't find his way out again. Knocked down a wire and many people saw it, so had to get out quick. Indians around the area appear very different, with flatter, wider-trimmed straw hats some with brightly-coloured tassels, men wearing knee-length coarsely-woven tunics with a long skirt underneath, and tied around with a belt, and no trousers. The women carry their belongings on their backs in a bundle secured with a band around their heads. Men make the women work very hard, many doubled over with the weight, one we saw carrying more than a donkey.

'Anyone coming upstairs in the bus would have a shock - Don and Joan have a machete next to their bunk, I have a saw under my bunk, Mike a hatchet under his mattress and Bern a sledge-hammer under her bunk.'

On July 10 they were stopped by the Army. Mike and Don descended from the cab at gunpoint and were frisked, much to their surprise.

On July 11, Sally wrote: 'We started to go up a steep hill at 6am. Bus crawled around first corner, stopped and started to roll back again. We emptied the water tanks and everyone got out and walked. Don drove about quarter way up the hill and then the bus refused to go any further. It was what we had feared - we had been offered a tow to the top for $20, but refused it, preferring to make it on our own. Panic stations to get blocks under the wheels to stop it rolling back over the side of the hill. I have never been so frightened for the bus.

Luckily a truck coming down the road loaded with men kindly turned round and towed up over the worst part. They declined $10 to take us to the top because their boss was waiting for them, and they were right in saying we would make it on our own, although admittedly a few of us watching were hoping and praying.'

And on towards Panama…

But first Sally was struck by the change in clothes as she encountered different types of Indians at a market at Chichicastenango – 'many Indians came down from the mountains for market day.

'Men, black woollen, long-sleeved shirts with colourful Spanish-type embroidery and tight knee-length pants, black Beefeater-type hats.

'The women wore extremely beautiful blouses, tapestry decorated or highly embroidered, some with a black satin rose inset into one shoulder.'

Dave recalled that as it was a Sunday lots of people were going to the Catholic Church, the inside of which was black with soot from candle flame and incense smoke.

A guard 'with a machine gun' opened a peep hole when they visited the British Embassy and they learned from the consular that the Brits were not well–liked because the province of Belize, which once belonged to Guatemala, was now being held unlawfully by the British, or so it was claimed. They were advised to park the bus outside the university sports building, where soldiers could keep an eye on it.

As they crossed the border into San Salvador on July 14 the bus encountered a low bridge in "no man's land."

They had a tried and tested way of checking the necessary clearance of the countless bridges they met on their travels.

Dave recalled later: 'We decided on a fishing rod to gauge the height of a bridge whilst we were in Florida. A new friend donated one. He laid it down on the ground at its full length and proceeded to measure it. Mike told him that was of no use. We needed to know the height. He was totally befuddled, while the rest of us curled up laughing.'

In San Salvador Sally noted: 'We had to completely let the tyres down and pile natives in the back, and scraped through. Bet we now have a few more leaks.'

Meanwhile the unrest continued. Dave's diary recorded: 'On July 14 we held a meeting. Got off to a good start when Bob and Jan said they were leaving at Panama. Mike also suggested the idea of leaving the bus at Panama and touring South Africa on our own. It will be thought about.'

The next day the bus smashed into a large neon sign and broke it. Luckily a man from the British embassy was nearby and smoothed things over.

As they passed through the city a crowd started cheering and they saw a woman with a large machete chasing a man down the street. He turned and threw a bottle at her, cutting her face, but undeterred she carried on and chased him into a police station! Sally recorded: 'There are six recorded murders every night in the city, how many unrecorded heaven knows!'

On July 19 the bus crew met Mike and Peggy Airey. Mike was manager of a silver mine worked by 220 men. Pumps ran all the time to prevent the eight levels from flooding and villagers did their washing in the artificial stream created on the surface. Mike arranged for some men to paint the bus roof with a sealer to stop leaks.

The following day the bus entered Honduras, with a permit for just two days travel. No El Salvadorian was allowed in the country, nor vehicles with El Salvador number plates, following a recent war between the two countries.

Sally reported: 'We could still see bullet holes in the walls. Actually the war seemed to have been a fiasco - the cause of it was said to be a football match which ES won, but underlying that was the fact that ES has a lot of people and not enough land, whilst Honduras has a lot of land and not enough people, so periodically ES residents infiltrate illegally onto Honduras land.

'They become extremely successful, prosperous farmers as they work very hard and use every inch of land, and this made local people jealous. The war, which was two years ago, lasted two weeks.'

On July 21 they entered Nicaragua. Sally wrote: 'The people are more lively than their neighbours, especially the children. Instead of just looking at the bus they bang the sides, shout and scream. They are quite friendly, the men blowing kisses at the girls. Bob got plenty of attention because of his blond hair.'

Ever conscious of the need to raise money to fund the trip, the group had picked up cheap whisky bottles with the aim of selling them. Several were sold to three English couples they met in Managua, a city of over 300,000 people.

Sally noted in her diary: 'Visited hotels and restaurants trying to sell Don and Joan's whisky. Outside a club two prosperous Nicaraguans came along and bought a bottle which they handed round to us, and they bought a meal, and then Don carried the half bottle that hadn't been drunk to the next cafe for them, but they soon forgot about it... with good reason!

'We had been drinking at an open cafe, tables on the pavement, and they were chatting Bern and I up, having told us they were not married, and then their wives turned up! Phew!

'One knocked all the things off the table, her husband ran for it, so she jumped in his car and tried to run him over! The other swung her handbag across her husband's face, then came after us.

'We explained that we didn't know they were married, and Bern said we weren't interested in married men and she was married herself, but the woman said she wasn't interested in what went on in our country, but in her country it was different. Luckily she thought we were Americans as she was going to report us to the Embassy in the morning. Don and Joan were most shocked."

On the plus side, Don still had his half bottle of whisky!

It is interesting to note that 17 months later, in December 1972, an earthquake destroyed much of Managua, killing between 3,000 and 7,000 people, and much of the international aid sent their never reached those who needed help, but was seized by the Government. Between 3,000 and 7,000 persons were killed by the earthquake, and some 15,000 were injured.

CHAPTER 20

The journey continued. Mike at one stage suggested that it might be worth considering leaving the bus at Panama, travelling across South America by bus and train, and then returning to Panama to ship the bus to Australia, but his idea gained little support.

While the crew debated whether to attempt to cross a river which was only a foot deep, but had a steep-sloped bank on the other side, the bus was surrounded by about 100 noisy kids. They decided to follow a longer, alternative route.

Sally noted 'a big bust up between Mike and Bob and Jan. I don't agree with either of them.'

Having crossed the border into Costa Rica on July 23, Mike left to travel to San Jose with an American to enquire about selling some advertising space on the bus to BOAC.

When the bus stopped at Sarchi, where there was a fiesta in progress, Sally and Bern went to a dance hall. Sally wrote: 'The men were not at all shy about dancing, the local hooch helped no doubt. As the only two 'Gringos' in the whole place we had a fabulous time, sometimes dancing with four or five men each.'

In San Jose, Don and Joan went around shops trying to sell some of the jewellery or tankards the group were carrying, but no luck as the Government had put a 60per cent tax on imports, making them too expensive to sell on.

Social life for the singles was good in San Jose, as Sally noted after visiting the El Baroco discothèque, 'plenty of nice-looking, well-behaved English-speaking men there, mainly students.'

Parking overnight near Cartage, the crew were informed by police that they had stopped on top of a village that had been buried by a volcanic eruption several years previously,

Sally's diary records: 'We were surrounded by people in cars, and even a coach brought people sitting five or six to a seat to have a look at us. We had trouble all day surrounded by hordes of kids, banging, shouting, trying to take the bus apart by any means. One had a table knife hacking away at our tyres, another a fork and spoon.'

More trouble was just around the corner. Early in August as they headed for the Panama border, Dave wrote: 'Back in Florida Don was nominated to hold the vehicle documents in his name. By the time we reached San José he was talking about putting people off the bus if he wanted to. Mike and I laughed at him and told him he couldn't do it, as it's a group vehicle. Today, however the problem re-emerged when Don said I would find out what he could do about putting people off the bus, with particular reference to me, when we reached Panama. It should be quite a stay in Panama.'

A lot of effort had gone into planning to get the bus on a ship to transport it to Colombia, so this was a crucial time. The Pan American highway does not continue further than Panama because of the Darien Gap. a huge region of primary rainforest that is dangerous (nowadays because of guerrilla groups and drug traffickers) and almost completely impassable, unless you had a guide, or maybe on a motorbike. It has been done. But not in a double-decker bus.

A major step forward was to actually pay for the bus to be shipped to Colombia.

Mike recalls: 'I negotiated with the Viceroy Cigarette Company for bus advertising and went ahead in both Costa Rica and Panama to try to obtain this.

'As David so pithily remarked "as new leader, Mike led from the front - usually 100 miles in front.!"'

Sally recalls: 'I remember walking through Panama City with the money from our cigarette company sponsors to pay the shipping line.

'It was a lot of money, and I think Mike was with me (Mike suggests Don and David were with them too), but opinion was that I was less likely to be mugged, because by that time to look at me you couldn't tell what nationality I was - with my dark hair, a deep suntan and wearing clothes that the locals wore and no jewellery, of course.'

The bus crossed the border into Panama on August 5, and Viceroy, which had purchased advertising space on the side of the bus, made it clear that they wanted the crew to travel through the city in the dark to their factory so no-one would see the bus without the adverts.

These would be placed on it the following day.

The company asked that the bus be driven to the village of Ocú to take part in an annual four-day harvest festival, which included playful competitions of dance and music.

The request was to show films across the village square from the top deck of the bus onto a truck with a large screen attached.

Mike recalls: 'They showed a few short Mickey Mouse films for children, then followed this up by of all things the World War Two film, The Dirty Dozen - a most unsuitable film I thought, but it seemed to go down well.

'Sally and Bernice enjoyed their evening by watching a wedding, where the bride and groom were paraded around the village streets under a canopy of straw matting held by four men. Everyone looked happy and excited and so the village passed another day of the Ocú festival.'

The bus having served its purpose returned to Panama City the following day.

It had been arranged that it would leave by sea for Colombia on August 28, with just one passenger allowed. The rest would have to fly or get another ship. Mike also investigated how much it would cost to take the bus by sea to Australia, and discovered it would save $2,000 if the bus was put in a box!

Sally met two US paratroopers from a nearby base and later went swimming with one of them in the French canal, an uncompleted length of the canal, wearing just her bra and pants. The other paratrooper went off by car to get some beer and never came back, which would have been OK had not Sally's clothes been in the car. It was getting dark and Sally's friend went off to phone a mate to collect them, and then he didn't come back, leaving her alone.

'I waited in the long grass and shivered, and the mosquitoes were having a feast on me, and I waited and waited. Over two hours later I heard a car and emerged from the grass, hoping Bern was looking for me, and she was. The paratrooper had got lost, looking for the French canal on the wrong side of the American bridge, and couldn't ask for directions because it was out of bounds for American servicemen,' wrote Sally.

On August 11, Bob and Jan left the group, to fly to New Orleans, as they had said they would. It was a blow for the remainder of the crew, now down from the original 11 members to just six – Mike, Dave, Sally, Bernice, Don and Joan.

As they waited for the day the bus would leave, life became a mixture of social events, often centred on the British or Americans living and working in Panama, and raising funds by using the bus as a centre for promotions. On August 24, Sally wrote: 'Joan fumigated bus as the previous night Bern found cockroaches in her bunk.'

It was also the night of a meeting when it was decided that everyone would use $200 of the funds to buy cameras, and $50 for film.

On August 25, Dave wrote: 'Serviced bus. Held another meeting. Flights booked for Tuesday. A local bus went in a ditch and we pulled it out, which was a nice change. Driver brought round six beers on his next trip.'

His diary recorded: 'Monday, August 30th 1971: Spent four days tying up loose ends. Got some fags and pipe tobacco from Benny and cashed travellers checks into dollar bills. Don, Joan and Gerald (a friend) returned in evening. They had been on the bus as it travelled to the docks, and stayed for a drink on the ship, the Rowanmore, and some of us went off to the pictures. Ship sails later tonight.

'Tuesday, August 31st 1971: Last visit to Embassy and bank before Benny picked us up and took us to the airport. Don and Joan had problems over their cameras, which were waiting there. Got Benny to take them into town. They got back to the airport just in time. Another five minutes they would have missed the plane.

'Flight was very comfortable and we landed at Midellin, Colombia at 4p.m. Customs were fairly simple and we were soon in town.

'Had to kick our heels for a while as there was no bus to Bogotá until later that evening. Had a meal in a local restaurant which was rather grotty and wandered around town for a while before boarding bus at 11p.m. Travelling time to Bogotá is about 14 hours.'

Sally and Mike were still with the ship. Mike (who didn't usually drive) drove the bus onto the nets, which then lifted it on to the ship – 'He was quite proud of himself,' remembers Sally.

They sat in the cabin of the First Mate, Cliff, drinking beer and watching the loading. 'Cliff is in his early 40s, acts much younger, great fun,' recorded Sally's diary.

'The Second Mate, Mitch, is gorgeous, handsome, dark curly hair, shy, my age. I could really fall for him.'

The captain was surprised to see the bus, having expected a two-ton camper rather than a 12-ton double-decker! He offered Sally the use of his cabin for the voyage. 'He said he would sleep on the couch, but as he did not promise not to try and share the bed, I politely declined,' she wrote.

In the end Mike slept in the pilot's cabin and Sally in the hospital.

Sally was a bit nervous about being the only girl on board with 42 men, so mostly stayed in Cliff's cabin, the coolest place, and drank his beer. She wrote in her diary: 'The captain walked into the cabin and laughed out loud when he saw Cliff and Mitch both fast asleep in chairs on each side of me, with me sitting on the floor reading All You Ever Wanted To Know About Sex, with 72 beer cans strewn around the floor. It was a good book, best I've ever read on the subject.'

CHAPTER 21

The ship arrived at Buena Ventura, Colombia, the following afternoon, but was not able to dock until 9.30pm, when the others joined Sally and Mike on board, prior to checking the bus through the customs. However, in the meantime there was a stabbing.

Dave's diary records: 'Wednesday September 1st 1971. On bus for nearly 16hrs reaching Bogotá at 3pm. Journey was tiring and for a lot of the way was over an all-weather road, which made it a bit bumpy. After getting off the bus we all walked down the road, about 100yds, to the next bus depot to check on buses to Buena Ventura.

'A local came up to Don and snatched his watch off his wrist. Don dropped all his cameras and chased him. He caught and hit him to the ground. When Don bent to retrieve his watch however hombre stabbed him in the side. Went to bus depot and they summoned a doctor who had a look. The wounds weren't deep and after treatment were covered by a plaster.'

Sally's diary added: 'Luckily Don is my build, plenty of layers of fat, otherwise the knife would have reached his kidneys and probably seriously wounded him. Crowd was in sympathy with Don; it's not often anyone manages to catch a thief.'

It took them three days to get through customs (Mike was negotiating to try to get them to reduce the $150 dock fees) and find diesel and they had to wait for an English ship to dock and then unload it in five-gallon drums.

Bern and Sally were ill. The roads were poor and progress slow, 300 miles in five days. There was a fuel strike in Colombia and they had been unable to get any apart from that from the ship. They put their reserve 15 gallons in and hoped they could find some soon.

On September 12, Dave recorded: 'Away early but the going is slow. Being Sunday there wasn't much traffic.

'There was a convoy of 14 trucks escorted by Military Police. They were carrying dynamite. Some very beautiful scenery on our route. The Andes are fantastic. Luckily it wasn't too hot so there wasn't too much haze around and one could see for miles."

The following day most of the group went into town to look at the market. Dave wrote: 'I stayed behind and adjusted the brakes. When Mike came back we went down to a garage and had our puncture repaired. Left Pasto about 1.30p.m. and got away on a good paved road. Made fair progress but shortly after Don took over driving one of rear tyres blew. Whopping great hole!!

'Put spare on and then carried on to Ipiales where we parked up for the night. Should cross the frontier tomorrow. Distance travelled: 50 miles.'

They reached the border at 9.30am, but couldn't cross into Ecuador because the archway across the road was too low. Sally said: 'We took an alternative route to the border, what a road!

'Took us all day to get under 10 miles, worst road so far, up and down, muddy, just wide enough for the bus, narrow bridges that I'm sure have never taken our bus weight before and most likely never will again. Thank goodness they did.

'When the border man saw us he just gaped, and let us straight through, still in shock. After all, he can only be used to seeing the odd smuggler and donkey or two. There were no customs and we have no entry permit!'

This could have been a major problem. They drove to Tulcán and parked up by the Customs office.

The Customs officials said they should have had a stamp from the Consul at Ipiales for entry and were going to send them back.

But they showed the officials papers from their files which said they didn't need it so the officials relented and let them in on tourist cards, though they would not stamp their passports.

Dave noted: 'Then we found out that Ecuador is not on our Carnet!! This could have been serious, but they stamped it anyway and let us in.'

Dave's diary recorded: 'Thursday, September 16th 1971: Away early but some local had half hitched our radiator cap. Progress was slow with lots of climbing. Road was either dirt or cobblestone. About 10.30p.m. arrived at Ibarra, which is about half way to Quito. The road we have been following is the new one under construction as the Pan-Am Highway.

'In Ibarra stopped to get a radiator cap and we were immediately surrounded by loads of people. Started selling postcards at 1 sucre (4d) each. Went like a bomb. A local chap took us to a market, where we met Amado Ruiz and his wife, Lucy, who, along with three kids and in laws, took us along to a market at San Antonio a nearby village. Saw some excellent wood carvings but didn't buy any.

227

'Went back to Amado's house and watched some of his people weaving cloth on the looms. Afterwards went to another village to see some shirts and dresses. Back at the house had dinner and then went to see some Indian dancing. All told it was a very interesting day. Sold postcards steadily during the day taking some $450.'

The following day they travelled on a very steep road about a mile north of the Equator. As Don took the bus around one corner the back off-side hit the road and tore open the back panel.

Two lines in the middle of the road marked the Equator. Soon after they had crossed it the bus ground to a halt on a very steep hill.

Sally wrote: 'Joan is now the official clutch adjustor, under Don's direction, because Don couldn't leave the cab for the bus would have rolled backwards, even though Mike and I were frantically wedging rocks under the wheels. Eventually, after a nerve-wracking hour, we made the hill.'

The following day she recorded: 'Everyone in a bad mood, terrible atmosphere.

On Monday, September 20th, Mike went downtown to see the people at Anglo Oil Co. He came back and said he'd got £150 for a three-day promotion at the international road race at Ibarra for the weekend. Later the company dropped to £100 but were providing the bus with free oil for an oil change and diesel in Ecuador.

Dave recorded: 'Yesterday I met Tony Thomson from London, who invited us to take the bus to his workshop where they would check over injectors and fuel pump. We went along and on the way were stopped by some German youths from Berlin. who are touring S.A. in a red VW bus. We had been hearing about them since our arrival in S.A. and we finally met up as is really bound to happen on this road.

228

They came with us to the workshop and stayed all day. Mechanics took the engine apart and found that two injectors were not working properly. This could account for your drop in m.p.g. We were averaging 6mpg at one point!'

They were not, of course, the only adventurers travelling around South America, but the most unusual was a 1934 Armstrong Siddeley, called Hamlet, crewed by a Cockney, Ron Rae, and his wife, Tove Rose, with their 10-year-old daughter. They had been driving the car, weighing one and a half tons, around South America, mostly Brazil, for three years, and hoped to settle in Canada.

The bus meets the German VW and Hamlet, the Armstrong Siddeley

'Their possessions are strapped on all side of the car, with many stickers,' wrote Sally.

'Tove, who is Danish, is almost completely paralysed from the waist down, and sometimes stays in the car for days on end. They have some amazing stories to tell, and Tove has already written three books about their trip.'

The bad feeling persisted. Dave recorded: 'Argument this morning. Don bitching as usual over silly points aimed at Mike and myself. I wanted to go to the Equator monument but everybody decided against it. I said I'd go myself on foot later in the morning. In the end we all went.

'Quite a nice monument and we were given a souvenir card to show we had visited the Equator. Pinned a bus card up on a visitors' board after we had all signed it.'

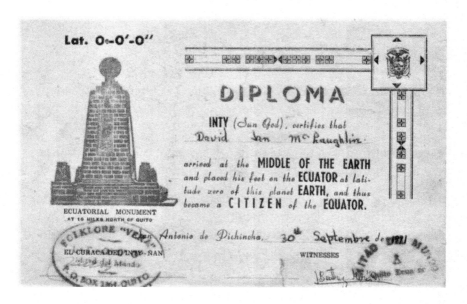

Lat. 0°-0'-0"

DIPLOMA

INTY (Sun God), certifies that
David Ian McLaughlin

arrived at the MIDDLE OF THE EARTH and placed his feet on the ECUATOR at latitude zero of this planet EARTH, and thus became a CITIZEN of the EQUATOR.

ECUATORIAL MONUMENT
AT 10 MILES NORTH OF QUITO

Antonio de Pichincha, 30th Septembre de 1971

WITNESSES

Anglo Oil were giving the bus free oil and diesel for the rest of the journey through Ecuador in exchange for the bus being seen on TV with their advertising on. They also wanted the bus to be seen at a car-racing meeting at Empalla.

On one occasion Bernice refused to go on the bus after it had been on a rickety bridge that bent right down as the bus passed over it. Sally recalled: 'It was only made from wooden planks and one or two of the supports had rotted away. The first time we went over Don drove while the rest of us walked behind still eating bowls of porridge.'

On their way they passed a bus that had gone over the edge of a cliff, with people being pulled out.

The race began at 12 midnight, stopped at 3.30 am due to an electrical fault in the pits, - allowing the group to get a little undisturbed sleep - and carried on again at 7am.

Sally's diary noted: 'There was a large crash and a car landed in the crowd and on top of a tent where people were sleeping. Four were killed and 18 injured, and we also discovered that 34 were killed when two coaches bringing spectators crashed off the road.

'During the race one car was burnt out, one landed in the lake, and some spectators were killed walking across the track - no crash barriers.'

Less important, but worthy of note: 'No toilet facilities, water, and we had very little gas.'

At this time Mike had to go to hospital suffering from a bad back, for which he was given medication, and Bern was unwell. Also, they saw six men trying to lift a donkey into a crowded passenger coach.

The journey continued...and so did the bickering. On Monday, October 4 1971, Dave's diary reads: 'Away early – 7a.m. Don moaning almost immediately about 'having respect for other people'. I don't understand him. Progress was very good with the road paved most of the way. One section was terribly muddy and the bus got filthy.

'At a checkpoint outside Santa Rosa we were warned about a low bridge at Arenillas. When we got there found a narrow bridge with two angled supports which we couldn't get under. The bridge has wooden boards for surface and also served as the railway bridge, which track ran down the middle.

'And so we forded our first river. Don and I went on a recce. I waded around and found a possible route, but Don decided the best way would be to dam the river, dig a channel and get rid most of the remaining water and then drive over. This caused harsh words again.

'Anyway we drove the bus down and ripped the rear panel in the process. At the river a crowd of interested spectators began to arrive to watch the crossing. A car showed us another way around, which was even better than the one I had in mind, so when a truck agreed to pull us out should we get stuck I shoved the green tube up the exhaust and started up.

I drove round in a wide circle and came out on the other side of the river bone-dry. The water didn't even cover the platform."

Sally noted: 'Have been warned to beware of sand dunes on the road. Tropical heat again. It's terrible, but Lima is only 800 miles away and we should reach it by the weekend. Mike still flat on his back, lying downstairs on the front seat in his pyjamas and gets all embarrassed when people look through the windows. Joan and I have sorted out a system, we take it in turns to cook and clean up.'

They crossed the border into Peru on October 8. Sally noted that the scenery had changed dramatically from what Dave had described as "flat and boring" to 'a blue-green sea on one side of the road and sand dunes on the other.'

There were, she said, red spider crabs dashing across the white sand and out at sea were local fishermen on tiny bamboo rafts with sails, competing for fish with diving pelicans.

CHAPTER 22

The following day they reached Sullana. On the outskirts of town was a bridge over the River Chira – it was a waterway that was to live in their memories for ever more.

The bridge had overhead struts in four box-type sections. Under the first three there was ample clearance on, but the last was too low.

The crew flattened the tyres, but were scraping the bars. Then the bus became stuck. The bridge had one-way traffic controlled by lights and police. It caused absolute chaos. On one tyre the valve had sheared off and the split rim fell off.

Since this holds the whole rim together, they had to change the tyre. The police got traffic moving past the bus, which made changing the wheel harder as it was on the side that traffic was passing. The jam stretched for miles.

Eventually they got the wheel on and then tried to get back off the bridge, filling the bus with enthusiastic schoolboys to bring the back down.

Dave recorded: 'Even then we were scraping badly. Still it had to come off so we forced it under. Once clear of the danger struts everyone breathed a sigh of relief. Reversed off the bridge to a garage where we put air in the tyres. Parked there overnight.

'A policeman came and took a note of all our names and passport no's plus carnet. Hope it's just for a report. Must say that they were all very good during the three hours we were on the bridge."

Sally's diary added: 'I was surprised how helpful the police were. They didn't fine us, and yet by their reckoning we had held up 300 cars.'

The following day, the local newspaper, the Correo, carried a photo of the bus stuck under the bridge, with a story about the chaos caused, caption: Omnibus Paralyzes Traffic!!

On Wednesday, October 6th 1971, the crew were up early and started sorting out tyres. Two had splits, and changed rims. A third required a new inner tube. They still needed to get the bus across the river.

A local bus driver took Dave to Amotape to look at the ferry service there for crossing with the bus. The river was too deep for fording and the road on the other side would present problems. However with a tow it might have been possible. The ferry consisted of two dugouts with a platform on top. It would just take the bus wheel base, though the back would overhang the water.

Dave recorded: 'I went back to the bus and told them about it. The local paper had been round and told them of another possible route, but when I went to find it the road was too difficult for the bus and locals said the river was too deep.'

The crew took the bus to Amotape, but on arrival decided against using the ferry. There were problems with boarding, and the road on other side. No tractor was available.

On the way to the ferry the bus had had a flat in the off-front tyre (new tube) again. An interesting point – it took about 10 minutes to do the tyre change. Everything went like it was a tyre change in a pit stop. Must have been all the practice.

Dave's diary for Thursday, October 7th 1971, reads: 'Went into Talara to see about the possibility of a boat down to Paita. Saw John Frisbee, who was in charge of boats with Teneco. They were unable to help us at the moment, but told us to go to Negritos to the Belco office.

'As we travelled to Negritos we were waved down by a young girl. She ran up asking where Sally was.

'Since it is not every day we get stopped in the desert by an unknown girl (English even) asking for one of us, we were quite surprised. Turned out to be Sandy Winterson, a girl who had been nursing with Sally at Southmead. She had read about the bus in the paper today, another article, which gave our names and she took off to find us.

'She took us into Negritos to the Convent, where she and another young English nurse, Sue Dunning, are staying. The sisters run a hospital, which was sent out from England. They were very friendly and overjoyed to see the bus and made us tea and cakes.'

The following day Bernice and Sally announced they were going to Rio.

Bernice had decided to return to the UK – and, of course, Roger - and Sally would act as escort and then check out the route to Santiago.

Bernice recalls she was determined to carry on after Roger left the bus, but, 'I eventually gave in nine months later (18 months into the trip) because I really wanted to see Rio de Janeiro.

'I bought a boat ticket that would take me from there back to Spain. When the bus got stuck in Peru and was going nowhere, I decided to leave and make my own way to Rio. Thankfully, Mike persuaded Sally, who was more worldly-wise than me, to accompany me.'

Sally noted that Don packed two of Bern's bags into one very large suitcase 'which I found impossible to carry any distance at all.'

Don and Joan were staying with the bus to carry out maintenance work, while Mike and Dave headed South to check the route.

Dave's diary recorded: 'Left bus at 12.30pm and took a Comit, a collective taxi, to Talara. From there took another to Piura. It cost $1 (U.S.) each but it is worth it to get on the Panam proper.

'Picked up a car within minutes, a Dodge Palara even. Took us from Piura to Truijillo in six hours. The driver, Pablo Tonoba, got us fixed up in a good, cheap hotel and took us out for a Chinese nosh in a local restaurant.

'The road South from Sullana is in very good condition, long, straight and flat with one small area of hills and 2 or 3 spots where it's been washed away. A couple of narrow bridges but no overheads yet.

'October 9: Left Trujillo by car to Chimbote. No problems on route. Chimbote is a fishing town and the smell is rather overpowering. It has also been flattened by the earthquake and signs are still visible as you drive out South. Got a lift in a Ford pick-up, which was going to Lima. Passed the tunnel way South near K240, but it looks OK. Main problem is a rail bridge near Pativilca, which could be close. Pressed to Lima and were dropped at Callao, Lima's port. Got in contact with the Lima cricket and football club, which is the biggest club in S.A. (English that is). They said to come over, so we did. Had an excellent evening and met some interesting people. Stayed in the club overnight.'

The following day, Mike – who had only recently recovered from illness - played a game of hockey as one team were a man short. Two minutes after bully-off he fell chasing the ball, and hurt his wrist.

He was taken to the Anglo-American hospital nearby and had it x-rayed - it was broken in three places and out of line. Doctors had to send for a specialist and he had an operation and came out the following day.

Mike recalls: 'My hand and wrist were broken and the surgeon put in three round metal rods that protruded a 1/4 of an inch beyond the four knuckles of my right hand. I was then stitched up and when I came around the next day it seemed like a club was fixed to my lower right arm.

238

'As we were only insured for £100 medical insurance, I was taken from the hospital that day by Dave to some people he had met at the Tennis club, Jack and Jo Lees, who hosted me for the six weeks while dressings were changed and the pins taken out. Only then could I return to the bus and much had happened by then."

Meanwhile, Bern and Sally were heading for Rio. The two girls hitched a lift to Talares, where, as Sally noted, they caused quite a stir – 'We didn't need the bus to draw a crowd, just stopped on the pavement and a huge crowd gathered.'

Eventually two men helped them tour the hotels until they found one that was not fully booked, the Hotel Peru, for 50 sols. The room consisted of two beds, a potty, one electric light bulb that didn't work, plaster falling of the ceiling and paint peeling off the walls. Bern was accosted in the toilet, but luckily Sally, her bodyguard, was standing outside and intervened. There was no water in the washroom.

They managed to get a lift with a kindly truck driver, who couldn't speak English, but bought them meals, and eventually they ended up at the same sports club as Mike and Dave, to discover that Mike had broken his wrist!

They picked up letters at the British Embassy, including one from me to Sal, which caused some consternation as it asked 'Did Sal think the bus with just three people could make it to Australia?'

As there were still five aboard, Sal wondered: 'What has Joan and Don written to him saying?'

Bernice received money sent from home and repaid money she owed to the bus. They carried on their journey. Local men were very hospitable, recorded Sally - a taxi driver not only carried them to a main highway free, but paid for their overnight stay in a nearby hotel.

On they travelled towards Bolivia, once catching the Rowanmore for a cruise down the coast, more often trying to hitch or getting local buses or taxis.

Meanwhile back in Peru, Mike and Dave were checking the route ahead IF they could get across the river.

Dave's diary recorded: 'Got a map from the Touring & Automobile Club and then went to the offices of the Ministry of transport and communications. Met the engineer who had written to us in Florida. He put me in touch with another chap and we pored over maps and books of the highway South. When we had checked everything went to another office and rechecked again. Road is clear except for two bridges, which we should be able to get under by flattening tyres.

'Back at the club (The cricket and social club) met the gang, Bill, Margie, Chick, Lydia and Mike and another lady, Jo Lees. Jo has a large house and after we had talked awhile she took Mike, Margie and I to her place for tea. She invited me to stay in her house overnight and it was a very pleasant evening.

'Thursday, October 14th 1971: Went to the Embassy and collected the mail for Don & Joan. Earlier the maid had brought me breakfast in bed, which was rather nice. Jo ran me to the bus station in the afternoon and I caught the bus to Talara leaving at 4pm. She had the maid fix me up with some tea and sandwiches to take with me. Journey should take 20 hrs.

'Friday, October 15th 1971: Arrived at Talara at 2.30pm. Went to Negritos and found bus parked at the Beclo yard. Earliest we can get away is middle of next week. There doesn't seem to have been much done on the bus. Back panel is still broken, roof still broken, nothing done on the electrical fault. Bernice's bunk has been changed and upstairs tidied, but that seem to be about all.

'Sunday, October 17th 1971: Had a terrible nightmare. Dreamt I had completely dried up and seemed to be unable to breathe.

'Knew what was happening and tried to wake myself up, but couldn't. Tried calling for Don and Joan, but couldn't even croak. Finally awoke, but it was a terrible dream."

Things could only get better. But they got worse. After considering various options, including trying to squeeze under another bridge, attempting to cross a shallow area, and driving the bus on rims, it was decided to have a go at crossing on a landing craft.

Dave's diary recalls: Tuesday, November 2nd 1971: 'To put it bluntly we blew it. I drove over the sand toward the landing craft. Don and I discussed how we should load the bus. This was essential because if we went on head first we would have to reverse off at the other end.

'We decided to reverse on and drive off. I drove forward and swung the bus around. Once I started to reverse the bus sank on the rear wheels. We tried to rock her out without success and the wheels bogged down further. Don and I had a look at the problem and I knew we would not get out under own steam. I pointed to a winch truck and suggested we use it to pull us out. Don would not have anything to do with it. He insisted we try rocking the bus again. I argued against it and he became very angry.'

When you get two strong characters at loggerheads, both of whom believe they have a way out of a difficult situation, both determined not to give in, and with no-one else available to damp the tension down, tempers flare, and bad decisions are made. This was a critical moment for the bus. One by one the drivers and mechanics had departed, namely Pete, Roger, and Bob, leaving just these two to keep the bus moving. Soon, there would be one.

Dave continued: 'I tried rocking the bus, but it went down further. Don tried putting rocks under the wheels, but it was no good. As I tried one rocking motion there was a loud bang. A winch truck got us out with a lot of effort and we got ready to try again.

'When we engaged reverse however there was a terrible noise. Thought the clutch was slipping, but when Don went to adjust it he noticed oil on the ground. The gearbox casing is broken. There may be more broken inside, because I don't see the casing accounting for the noise, though it could if it was touching the gears. Had a tow back to the Belco yard and went up to Mike's for a beer and dinner. Tomorrow we start work on removing the gear box.

'Wednesday, November 3rd 1971 - As feared, the reverse gear shaft is broken on its mounting. A 6" square piece of the casing is also broken completely and there are on or two running cracks. It may be very difficult to fix the gear mounting as it has to be very exact. Before dropping the gear box we shall try and get an expert to have a look and give us an opinion on the extent of the damage and whether it can be replaced.'

The bus was stuck in Peru and it was inevitable that the rows were continuing

On Saturday, November 13th 1971 Dave recorded: 'Started up and moved the bus. When Don engaged reverse there was a horrible noise, bus didn't move and the epoxy broke again. Parked up again and a big row started. I wanted to try and patch it with some of our own stuff, which we have on board. Don started shouting that it was a stupid idea, wouldn't work, wasn't going to work, he wasn't going to allow it, it was his bus, etc, etc. Mike intervened and in the end I got to try it my way. Cleaned off the cover and applied the epoxy. It took and looks reasonable. Drove around town for a couple of turns to try it out. Did not try reverse. There are one or two leaks, which I shall try and fix tomorrow.

'During the argument this morning Don got round to his usual argument of he owned the bus and could throw people off. He produced a letter from Roger in which Roger told him this, specifically aimed at me, and that he would do it in Australia. I told him not to bother waiting, we'd do it in Lima.'

And leave he did: on Friday, November 19th 1971 the diary records: "Nothing much today. Usual moans. In the evening Don, Mike, Chris (Chris Skirton who had been in on Don and Joan's original trip and had met up with the group in Panama from Australia) and I called for the girls and went to the flea pit and saw a Swedish film. After went to the bar for a beer and decided to leave with Chris the following day and get away for a while. We intend to head for Huaraz and then Lima."

Dave received a letter from the bank in Panama with a Bank Giro for $1000 U.S. in response to a letter he had sent from Negritos. He had it changed into travellers cheques.

Dave recalls: 'Mike was a bit upset when I said I was off on Monday and a bit mad when he realised I had the money. Still not much could be done about it. Told Don and Joan I was off. They didn't say a word, which amazed Mike. Later they started ticking however and, using Mike as a go between, we got things sorted out and in writing."

And there, with the bus still on the wrong side of the River Chira and of the original crew, only Mike, Don and Joan left, Dave's diary ends.

CHAPTER 23

The bus was now down to one driver/mechanic, Don. As hard-working, determined and skilled as he was, the odds must have been against the remaining members of the group progressing much further, even if they managed somehow to cross the river. Australia must have seemed a long way away.

Meanwhile Bernice and Sally, still heading for Rio, had more adventures including hitching a lift from two men in a lorry, who were so obviously attracted to them that they were invited to their home to see their pigs!

Bern recalls: 'We were hitch-hiking across South America. I found it so daunting that when we reached La Paz in Bolivia, I decided not to carry on and rather selfishly traded my boat ticket in for a flight from Lima to London, leaving poor Sally to find her own way back to the bus – or not (Sorry Sal!).'

Sally's diary noted: '18th October: She will be home in time for her younger brother Brian's wedding, on Saturday. I'll miss her to travel with.'

Sally started her journey back across South America and then back to the bus, nervous, but determined – 'It's a frightening thought having to travel on my own.'

She recalls: 'I only spoke pigeon Spanish, but used to use my diary to make conversation, because it had postcards in it from different countries.'

On one occasion she travelled in a cattle truck, sleeping in a hammock, while several men slept on boxes and bags. In Brazil, she noted the train was 'much better than the English ones.

'Travelled second class, waiter came round with coffee, beer, brandy, soda and even hot dinners, floor cleaned about six times a day.

'Most people I met were really kind and helpful and I only had one bad experience, but I survived.'

That episode included sleeping in a broken-down shack with no door and waking to find her handbag had been stolen, along with her camera, glasses, rings etc. Luckily, she had been sleeping on a second bag with passport and some money inside.

Two good drivers took her on to Porto Alegre. She noted: 'Every single driver I get proposes to me. It's very difficult to explain to them why I can't and won't remain in Brazil or even get married.'

On November 26, Sally was in Lima and just starting to panic, because the British embassy had no word on where the bus was, when quite by chance she met Dave and his friend, Chris, and they were able to reassure her that the bus was probably still in the same place.

She made it back to the bus at Negritos early in December - Sally recalls: 'Mike and Dave told me that they were surprised to see me, as they never expected me to survive the trip!'

They were still there in January having spent a very enjoyable Christmas Eve with local friends and a quiet Christmas Day recovering.

They had a letter from the company that made the bus back in the UK offering to send a new reconditioned gear box for £100, but the crew felt it would be impossible to get it into Peru. There was also an offer from a local oil company, Labitas Oil, to take the bus and passengers back to England free but 'that would be giving up. But it is nice to know the offer is there as a last resort,' wrote Sally.

Matters came to a head in early February when the group thought they had found a way to get across the river on a raft, but then at the last minute the oil company providing the raft said it could not get into the berth because the high tide had washed a sandbar on to the beach, preventing the bus getting off the raft.

Instead, they advised that an attempt should be made to cross the river by raft at another location.

'None of us wanted to go or was happy about the idea,' wrote Sally. 'But Belco insisted they had carpenters there to build a ramp to get us up on to the raft, a caterpillar tractor to help, and a truck and men to help as well. We couldn't refuse, if we had it would have looked as if we preferred to help ourselves, even when help was given to us.'

They arrived at the river to see the caterpillar tractor stuck on the raft in the middle of the river 'and that is lighter than us.'

Men swarmed in to push the raft back to shore, the ramp had been built, and strong boards were laid down to enable the bus to cross the shore to the raft.

Everything was ready but, said Sally: 'I had a strong premonition that something would happen and packed into my bags everything I considered most valuable, money log books, scrapbooks, and took them out of the bus. Joan packed all her valuables, including souvenirs and films, into boxes and put them downstairs ready to grab if anything happened.'

The raft was very primitive; wooden planks anchored over two small rowing boats. Gradually the bus was eased on to the raft. When the front wheels reached the boards they creaked worryingly, and the caterpillar tractor piled sand between the bank and the raft to support them.

'Once the bus was on the raft it took about 40 men pushing with all their strength for 25 minutes to ease the raft away from the shore," noted Sally.

'Don and Mike were in their swimming trunks, but most of the other men were stripped down to the waist in their underpants – I have never seen so many baggy, ragged brownish-coloured underpants in my life.'

Progress was extremely slow at first, but once the raft reached the middle of the river the current was too fast for the men to control it.

'After a frightening minute or two they seemed to regain control of it and shoved it the right way, but the bus was slipping backwards because the back boat was slowly filling with water. A man jumped into the boat and began to bale furiously, but to no avail, the boat slowly but surely filled with water and before most people realised what was happening the bus slid gently backwards into the water, so quickly that Don was unable to retrieve Joan's valuables,' wrote Sally.

'Joan immediately jumped in from the bank and attempted to swim to the bus, but even though she swam with all her strength the current started to pull her downstream away from the bus. I was afraid for her for a moment, but she was able to reach the bank safely.'

Don and Mike went out to the bus by rowing boat, opened the rear door and found that the water had already filled the bus to a level half-way up the back stairs.

They cleared the top deck of personal possessions and papers from the filing cabinet, placing them inside sleeping bags and handing them out of the rear upstairs window to people in the boat. Joan then made another attempt to swim out and this time succeeded, to the cheers of the watching crowd.

The following day three attempts were made to pull the bus out, but the bus had settled down into the sand and water nearly filled the top deck with the result that the wires were not strong enough.

The third time a thick wire rope was fetched from a nearby village and this managed to pull the bus around to a more level angle, but not pull it out.

Two days later, Sally's diary recorded: 'At last the bus has been towed out of the water by two caterpillar tractors with a heavy wire

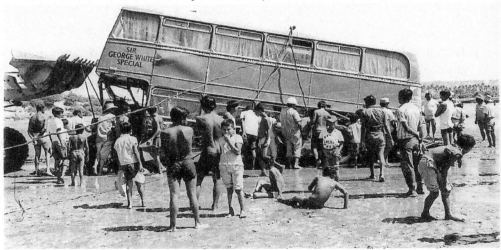

Sally noted: 'There is no cab and the back has been torn away, and it just rests on the ground, which makes it even more difficult for the boys to salvage the tools, spare parts etc from under the downstairs seats.

'A guard was left overnight, but people were stoning the windows and would have stoned him if he hadn't got out of the way.

'Everything left was taken, all the fixtures, seats, tables, woodwork, laminate, bunks, cupboards; they even tried to remove the windows, frames and panels of metal from the side of the bus.

'What had taken us four months to put in, took one night to get out!'

One 11-year-old boy drowned during the salvage attempt, having fallen into the river with his brother, who was saved. Don had made friends with them the previous day. It was a terrible shock to everyone.

The boatman in charge of the raft told the local press the bus rolled backwards because the brakes were not put on, not because the back boat was sinking. 'He must have been bribed,' noted Sally.

In fact, when the wreckage of the bus was towed to Piata, the badly-damaged back end resting on top of the truck, Don had to release the brakes to enable the surviving front wheels to turn.

Belco, the oil company, helped the group as much as they could, letting them have a driver to run them around and translate for them as they worked out what to do next. 'People in Negritas are being absolutely fabulous,' wrote Sally. 'We moved our possessions into a Belco house, it's large and nice.'

The bus was signed off as a wreck. Unable to travel any further, Mike left on February 24 to travel to Lima and inform the embassy what had happened.

On March 6 he contacted the group from Lima to say they could all get a ship back to Barcelona leaving in two days' time, fare $384 each, and wanted the number of the bus passbook to get the money out.

Sally wrote: 'There are many reasons against going; problems with getting us and our stuff down to Lima in time; how to get it economically from Barcelona to Bristol. Fares high etc.'

There was also strong feelings about why they were not travelling back home on a Lobitos oil tanker, another option - Mike claiming the company had refused to take them, although Sal believed there had never been a firm arrangement.

Don decided to fly down to Lima and see what was happening, but while the plane was at Trujello the engine caught fire.

Sally wrote: 'People panicked and ran for the doors which were closed. Chaos ensured, but as there was no way of getting out, Don stayed in his seat and calmly surveyed the scene. Soon the fire was extinguished and everything was well for the rest of the journey.' She added that passengers were always worried of a crash because the planes were overloaded and not properly maintained.

Sally's diary also noted, on March 11, that there was a fantastic sky, with 'a complete rainbow around the sun and another one upside down in the sky, with both ends pointing upwards away from the mountains.' She said she hoped it was not an ominous sign, as many local people feared.

Shortly afterwards a period of torrential rain began, including thunderstorms which terrified the local people, and in a very short time many villages were flooded and mud slides were causing a problem.

On March 23 Sally wrote: 'The rumour is that there is only two days' food supply left in the Talara area. Many men are flying their families down to Lima. Already infections are spreading and babies are dying.'

She added: 'A new law was passed at the beginning of the month – no meat for the first 15 days of each month! This is to encourage people to eat fish because there is a shortage of meat.'

Sally had nothing but praise for the local people and the oil company, who were being so helpful, in spite of the difficult weather and health problems, but sadly many people were upset by an article in the Peruvian Times, from an interview with Mike, which failed to express thanks to any of them.

Mike comments: "It's apparent that I had a story in the Peruvian Times, which did not do justice to the help and assistance given by the Belco team and their families. If this so, then this was a severe lack of judgement on my part as it seems from Sally and Bernice's notes that they had been very hospitable indeed."

Don returned from Lima with the good news that Lobitos had generously said they would take them home to England, departing March 26 by oil tanker, via the Panama Canal, taking 16 to 25 days. Don and Mike had sought help from the British Embassy and the trip was arranged after many meetings.

Sally was delighted: 'It will be luxury for us, comfortable cabins, plenty of good food and fruit, swimming pool, going at a good time of year for plenty of sun.'

The journey was delayed, but on April 3 the four remaining crew members, Don, Joan, Mike and Sally, loaded a large crate, bags and boxes containing their belongings on to a lorry, and despite difficulties caused by heavy rain and flooding, which had blocked many roads and caused a shortage of food across the area, they reached the docks and were carried to the tanker in a small boat.

Even then there was one last drama. Don recalled that they could only reach the tanker by the small boat, and when they pulled alongside a crane lowered a net to collect their luggage.

'As it lifted up, one case fell out into the sea – guess who's it was, yes, mine,' he said. 'I didn't think twice, just leapt into the water and swam to it. By that time it was sinking, and I held onto it until the boat moved round and hauled me aboard. Of course, everything in the case was ruined.

The ship, the El Lobo, or Wolf, carried a crew of 40 men, and with Sally and Joan there was only one other girl on board, the Third Engineer's wife. It was, recalls Sally, as luxurious as they had hoped.

The boat sailed into Liverpool on April 15th, 1972, just a few days short of two years since the bus was loaded onto the boat to Montreal at Avonmouth.

THE ACTUAL ROUTE TRAVELLED BY THE BUS

27 April, 1970 - Bus departs Avonmouth, Bristol, by ship to Canada

5 May, 1970 - Bus arrives in Montreal, Canada

23 May, 1970 - Bus enters USA at Buffalo, New York State

12 June, 1970 - Bus enters Mexico, Central America, at Nuevo Laredo

30 June, 1970 - Bus re-enters USA at San Diego, California

28 October, 1970 - Bus re-enters Canada at Vancouver, BC

6 December, 1970 - Bus re-enters USA at Buffalo, New York State

17 June, 1971 - Bus re-enters Mexico

8 July, 1971 - Bus enters Guatemala

14 July, 1971 - Bus enters El Salvador

20 July, 1971 - Bus enters Honduras

21 July, 1971 - Bus enters Nicaragua

23 July, 1971 - Bus enters Costa Rica

05 August, 1971 - Bus enters Panama

02 September, 1971 - Bus enters Colombia, South America, by ship from Panama

15 September, 1971 - Bus enters Ecuador

04 October, 1971 - Bus enters Peru

05 October, 1971 - A Bridge Too Low at Sullena

02 November, 1971 - Gear box broken boarding landing craft

20 February, 1972 - Disaster crossing the River Chira.

THE JOURNEY ENDS

CHAPTER 24

What happened to the crew? Sadly Joan, Don and Roger have all died.

Joan, the motherly Mrs C, who worked for Standard Life for 24 years, died in 2007. "I miss her like mad, and even now I sometimes talk to her in her chair, call her Missus like I always did," Don said when we visited him in 2018.

Don lived on near Bristol for many years, retained his stature, despite the fact he was 83 when we last met. He had a great memory and remembered all the bits you hoped he had forgotten!

When he and Joan returned to England they stayed with Joan's mum for a while.

'Then I managed to get a job driving lorries during the M5 construction, which paid great money and got us back on our feet," he recalled.

He died two or three years ago.

Roger had a long fight against cancer, which he was determined to win. In the face of his optimism no-one else dared to think differently, but he succumbed in July, 2015.
.
"He was the most optimistic man I ever met," said one mourner at his funeral.

I was honoured to be a pall-bearer, He was an inspiration to all who met him, and when he left the bus we were leaderless. In my opinion, we never recovered.

Before he died, Roger had written: 'When I left the bus in Florida I had intended trying to go to Ruskin, but got a job as a full-time official with NUPE.
'I became area officer in Hampshire and the Isle of Wight and on my many visits experienced John's IOW car ferry steak and kidney pies - undoubtedly the best in the world!'

As previously noted, Roger went on to have a distinguished career as a trade union leader and in negotiations over the Northern Ireland Peace Deal.

He once told me that in talks between his committee and Ian Paisley and his Protestant allies, Mo Mowlem, the indefatigable Northern Ireland Secretary at the time, became so fed up with their antics that she said: "Mr Paisley, Fuck Off!" And he did.

Bernice said: 'It was a challenge he enjoyed, prompting Peter Hain to say of him that he could persuade people to do things which they ended up thinking had been their own idea.
'He enthused people to believe in their abilities and better themselves, especially women.'

The Guardian obituary read: 'Roger became the acceptable face of trade unionism at the end of the bitterly-divided 1980s, as the spokesman for ambulance staff in their largely-successful six months of industrial action. He went on to build a reputation as one of the most constructive negotiators of his generation. Poole's homespun style, aided by his West Country burr, could not disguise a fierce commitment to low-paid workers, while his patient capacity to build trust and find a way through complex negotiations later led to his appointment as chairman of the Northern Ireland Parades Commission (2005-09). Subsequently his constructive, often humorous, presence was in demand as a patient behind-the-scenes fixer helping to resolve industrial relations conundrums.'

He and Bern had two children and three lovely granddaughters. In 1993 they had bought a house in France that he said became "a bit of a money sump, but well we love it."

"Looking back it is quite clear that our lives would have been very different if we hadn't put that advert in the Bristol Evening Post.

"P.S. Bern has not read this so it will be good to see how much she contradicts me, something she has become an expert in over the last 46 years."

BERNICE:

'On my return to England we started married life properly in a tiny rented room in a shared house in Southampton. where Roger was employed by the union, NUPE.

This was 1971 when buying houses was a nightmare, a time of gazumping, when we actually sat in people's front rooms and tried to outbid each other on the house we were trying to buy.

"We eventually bought a house at the top of the market. Roger rang me to tell me he had just bought the house (no time for me to see it first). We spent 18 months improving the house, during which time we had our first child Jason, in April 1974. The same month my dad was made Lord Mayor of Bristol. Within a year Roger had been promoted to Brum, but as we now could not sell our house - the market now being in decline - Roger spent the next six months commuting. We eventually bought a house in Droitwich and within two weeks of moving in my dad died. My mum went into a deep depression and the end result was that we had a granny flat built for her and she happily lived there with us for the next 30 years until she died in 2011.

'After our daughter, Jessica, was born in '75 I decided we needed a playgroup and so set one up in the local community centre. This occupied me for the next five years or so, but during this time I had returned to my first love – my sewing machine - and made my own and the children's clothes as well as soft toys and wooden sewing boxes. A selection of these were loaded into the old pram and, usually with a hobby horse sticking out of the top, my mum set off on a Friday morning to walk to the local WI market to sell what she could for me. A local hotel owner asked if I could help her refurbish the hotel by upholstering the furniture and making new curtains, etc.

'So started my next enterprise, a workshop in the garage (albeit a small-scale business, but one which continues today).

'We had always hoped to get a small holiday home in Wales and in 1992 when Roger was left a small inheritance, we looked for a place to renovate. The prices were out of our price range, but I did spot an advert for a house in France, so we started to look over there.

'We found a 400-year-old fermette south of the Loire and have spent 16 years renovating it, turning a small barn into a lovely two-bed gite for our dotage.

'Two years' ago I finally lost the last of my parakeets, which I have enjoyed breeding in a large garden aviary for the last 30-odd years – and I still miss them.

'Roger's mum's mum also died in 2011 at the age of 99. Roger retired for the second time – he first retired 10 years ago at which time we bought a motor home, which lives in France, and when we could, we would set off touring around Europe or Morocco, reliving our previous life as members of Omniworld. And to keep me out of mischief I am rather late in life struggling to learn the piano but my left hand still doesn't know what the right hand is doing.'

DAVE:

'Life on the bus was always interesting even if there were tough times and disagreements. We worked through them. As a result we all formed a bond, which continues to hold us together some 50 years after it ended. Don and I had a big disagreement at the end. It was too serious for me to stay on the bus and so, like others before me, it was time for me to go.

'I travelled to Lima to stay with friends whilst I got reorganised. I determined to make the most use of the opportunity now available to me and planned a route to travel from Lima to Rio De Janeiro. First port of call was Cuzco and the ancient city of Machu Picchu.

Next I travelled to Lake Titicaca. Visiting a floating reed island was fascinating. The bus to La Paz, Bolivia broke an axle and we spent a night huddled in the cold before the morning bus arrived. It was full but we all got on board anyway.

I spent Christmas 1971 in the company of fellow travellers attending midnight mass in the cathedral.

'Onward to the Falls of Iguazu at the borders of Bolivia, Paraguay and Argentina before a long train and bus journey to Rio. Walking up Mount Corcovada to see the statue of Christ the Redeemer; time on Copacabana beach and admiring a city that was very beautiful and yet had such poverty alongside.

'From Rio I caught a ship to Portugal and travelled through Europe to London. My parents had moved from Bristol and were living in London, so I tracked them down about 10pm.

'It gave them a surprise. I returned to Bristol shortly before everyone else got home as well. I joined the Civil Service working at the Department of Health and Social security, which proved to be a job with lots of variety and interest. I even managed several transfers, one to the Outer Hebrides and later to Orkney. Mike and Peter Conway were firm friends and we did a lot together for many years. Sally passed me in the street one day, but responded to my call. Joan Coles answered a phone call I made to a company one day and did a double take at my name. We renewed our friendship.

'Everyone else was out of contact for a very long time. We had a bus crew reunion and gathered at Roger and Bernice's home. It was a splendid evening. Bob was visiting from Australia and John and his wife were present. Jan and Pete were absent as they had lost touch with us over the years. My daughter was a little perturbed when she went to the loo and there was a photo of the bus and crew on the inner side of the door!'

SALLY:

'On my return from the bus trip I went back to nursing and after two failed marriages I lived with my husband, Dave, for 24 years in a mobile home in a small park in the West Country. I am lucky to have a prime spot in the park where two rivers meet. Thus, without a mortgage we were able to afford to travel more.

'My parents and brothers have lived in Ontario in Canada for many years, so we have visited frequently also taking the opportunity of travelling from there to many parts of the USA. My parents were also Snow Birds and had a mobile home in Florida and in fact it was here that Dave and I were married. My second husband had introduced me to the jazz scene and Dave and I visited as many jazz festivals around the country as we could.

'Mum lives in Ontario and is still very active, managing to do a great deal of travelling. She and my dad retired from farming 21 years ago.

'I never had children, but have enjoyed a very extended family, including my nieces and nephews in Canada as well as children and grandchildren from Dave's first marriage."

Sally spends a lot of time in Canada near her mother, now well into her 90s, who recently (as I write) went into a nursing home.

BOB:

He married Jan and they moved to New Zealand 'because it was where people built Ferro cement yachts in their back or front yards and we thought that we might do similar, and continue our nomadic adventures. Thus began my second apprenticeship, in boat-building and sailing, at Auckland.

'Little did we realise at the time it being the best place in the world, and still is, in the art of all boat-building and sailing. They are in my view the best most fanatical sailors on par with the French.

Self- taught ten years later in 1982 after plenty of blood sweat and tears, we departed for remote Pacific islands on Rock of Ages, our floating footpath yacht. Sailing with no GPS, or communication crap in the wake of Chichester, not for glory but personal satisfaction. We sailed the 'milk run' between NZ and Australia via the South Pacific islands on a number of occasions over the next few years, living aboard our yacht.

'More than 20 years later I'm still a wayward sailor living in the South Pacific region. I have another love in my life a catamaran, which I built and which I sail alone, with mother nature my companion. Life is an adventure. Life should be a holiday. Life is what you make it.'

He recalls: 'When I was 12, teacher asked me, in front of the whole class, where is Tasmania? I said I didn't know. But, when I was told, I never forgot it.

'Then, 1986, when we were in Brisbane, we were married, on the mono, Rock of Ages, and went to Tassie to put the lifts in the hotel, that overlooks Constitution Dock, where the Sydney-Hobart race boats dock after the race. While in Tassie, my marriage broke up. Then, in 2013, I damaged Bobzaway, when in Tassie! What do they say, "never go back?" Ha, Ha!'

After a year or so of indecision he undertook the repairs to the boat and is now occasionally back on the high seas, spending Christmas and New Year moored in Sydney Harbour within view of the Opera House. He is particularly fond of sailing with the whales that gather off the eastern shore of Australia.

Bob, now a confirmed Aussie and bachelor, said: 'Since launching the boat, 10 weeks ago, I'm living on board, loving it. My house? It's just used as a workshop.'

MIKE:

"Hitching a ride on a tramp oil tanker back from Peru to Liverpool with three remaining fellow travellers, I enjoyed the life at sea and was determined to continue travelling. It took a further two years to realise the dream, during which I worked as head chef in a country club in Caerphilly in South Wales, before being promoted to General Manager.

'Again desperately unsettled and with itchy feet I applied to join the Merchant Navy and at last was able to get round the problem of being issued with MN Card and with this was able to apply for a post at sea. I was appointed Catering officer on the London Statesman. I joined in Lorient in France bound for USA. The ship's Master was a Captain Nelson!

'During one of my leave times in late July 1978 my old bus buddy, Dave, took me to his social club and I met Sheila. We were engaged after just two months and married in October.

'In November. 1978 Sheila and I joined a 250,000-ton tanker in Greece to begin our six-month honeymoon. Our second voyage in 1979 took us 800 miles up the Amazon deep into the jungle to pick up bauxite for Thunder Bay in Canada. After Canada we ended the voyage in Houston, Texas, and travelled the route of the bus from Los Angeles to Kings Canyon and Kings River before heading to San Francisco and back to Los Angeles to fly home courtesy of Freddie Laker .

'After 15 years at sea and going round the world many times, including a voyage around Cape Horn and seeing lots of waves, I came ashore, eventually joining the then Women's Royal Voluntary Service as Bristol hospital coordinator and then taking over as the South West Regional Hospital Manager and took retirement in 2001.

'Not ready to become a a trainee pensioner I joined the local branch in Nailsea of Iceland as White Goods Appliance Manager, staying for six years, gradually reducing my working weeks, so I could have a long winter break in Spain. I took full retirement on Christmas Eve 2008."

Sheila and Mike wintered on the Costa Blanca in an apartment for many years, running around in a Spanish car and spent several months travelling to Galicia and the Basque countries.

But in recent years Sheila, following a fall in Spain, has been living in a care home, with Mike visiting her each day. He is now able to take her out in a wheelchair.

JAN AND PETE

Sadly of these two I have no news; they have not been in contact.

ME:

I was restless when I returned to England. I was back working on the Isle of Wight County Press for a few months and by sheer chance as I made a telephone call to request a journalist to cover a court appearance by an island man, I spoke to an old mate, Richard Ingham, at the Luton News, and he said they had a vacancy.

I moved there, and had eight great years, mostly because I met my wife, Nancy, before we moved up to Derbyshire. She was an air hostess, who had a similar sense of adventure (she travelled on her own in Canada and Ireland), and she shared a great many of my interests, socialising, travel, walking. As I had expressed the desire for earlier in this book, I had found the ideal person to share life's experiences with, the love, the ordeals, parties, joys, sorrrows and hardships.

It would have been great to have had her with me to see the breathtaking views of the Californian national parks (we did however enjoy the Autumn colours of the Fall in New England many years later!).

The Fickle Finger of Fate is a miraculous digit. Had I not left the bus, returned home, joined the County Press, made that phone call to the Luton News, and gone to a pub for a lunchtime pint (or two) with Chalky White, I would have never have met my wife there. We have two great kids and five boisterous grandsons.

That reminds me of another story. A few months after my fateful meeting with Nancy, Chalky White, with whom I played tennis at lunchtimes (when I wasn't in the pub), left the Luton News.

On the day before his departure a farewell card came round to be signed, and I wrote: "Next time throw your balls up higher" – a reference to his poor serve. About an hour later another card came round to be signed. "Who's card is this?" I asked. "It's for Chalky," said a colleague. Oh, horror – the first card I had signed was for a chap in advertising I didn't even know! I often wondered what he, or even his wife/partner (let's be politically correct), thought!

When I left the Luton News one of our reporters, Dave Renwick, later to become a famous TV writer (one Foot in the Grave etc) designed a farewell card with a cartoon image based on an interview I had carried out with members of the local Gay Club. "We always knew you would marry a Nancy!" it proclaimed. We still have it.

I worked as a reporter and page planner on the Sheffield Star for nearly 30 years, became hugely popular dishing out freebies as travel editor (I travelled a lot until I became bored with it, missing the wife and family). With the help of Nancy and friends I launched my own community magazine Wings, of which I am tremendously proud, so that I could go back to the grass roots of reporting and writing.

Now I enjoy retirement, golf (sometimes with another Chalky White!), walking in the wonderful Peak District, holidays abroad, and looking after the grandkids.

If learned anything from the bus trip it was to cherish the family - Nancy, of course, son Nathan and his wife, Mel, daughter Emma and husband Matt and the grandsons, Tom, Josh, Max, Oliver and George, and Nancy's and my surviving siblings - they are always there for you when you need them, even though our kids may be a worry (like I was to my dear Mum and Dad). And good friends will always stay in touch.

Travel broadens the mind and should be encouraged at every opportunity, but the best thing about it is getting back to the family and friends. If I was 27, would I do the same trip today? It would probably not be possible.

The spread of terrorism means that countries are red-hot on security and every traveller has to have the right visas and permits. We would not now be able to thwart the height restrictions on our double-decker in the way that we did then.

Mexico and the Central American countries seem to be far more dangerous places, when you travel off the beaten track because of gang violence associated with drug smuggling.

On the plus side for independent travellers, it is now a lot more convenient to be able to find out where you are and which route to take via satellite navigation, and with the internet and mobile phones you can keep in touch with anyone from almost anywhere.

It is an interesting thought that, although the launch of rockets carrying astronauts to the Moon has always been regarded as Man's greatest achievement in space, and caused huge interest at the time, I'm certain that the placing of communication satellites around the Earth via almost unnoticed rockets that took off from Cape Canaveral and other space stations across the world, has had a far greater influence on our lives today.

As a matter of interest, once back in the UK I never ever smoked pot again. Maybe it was because it was not so easy to get hold of. Maybe I grew out of it. Or perhaps it was being back in the comforting embrace of warm, dark beer! Now, with all the micro-breweries that have sprung up in recent years, I drink less of it but enjoy it even more, particularly cold beer! A pub near us has 11 real ales on every night. I plan to buy several bottles of Newcastle Brown Ale for Christmas.

Once back in the UK I soon had asthma again, but medication controls it unless I mess with cats or rabbits. I recall that Playboy bunnies had a much more pleasant effect! But enough of that – I should know better at my age!

The bus crew have had several reunions in over 50 years, but I don't keep in regular contact with them apart from Bernice. You can't put a crowd of strangers together in confined quarters for so long and expect them to become lifelong pals.

Now I am a lot older I get free bus travel thanks to a bus pass, but rarely use it because of Covid. Strangely before that I never became bored with bus travel and I loved travelling on the upper deck!

THE BUS:

Lastly, what happened to the bus? After the wrecked bus was returned to Negritos, the Peruvian customs pointed out that the bus had been allowed to enter the country as a tourist vehicle, and if it remained in the country it was liable for importation tax. This would have cost a lot of money and plans were made to solve this.

The main plan was to use an oil company boat to take the bus out to sea and push it overboard. In the end it was decided to gift it to the Peruvian government, and it was last seen by the crew lying broken on a jetty. Some years later when Mike worked in the merchant navy a fellow officer told him that on his last voyage he called in at Negritos and the wreck was still there.

Sally heard that the shattered remains now lie in a scrap-yard on a cliff top near a small village in Peru. No doubt it is bent and rusted and bears no resemblance to the vehicle that was our home for so many months over 40 years ago. But it may live on in the memory of local people, who talk about the red bus that fell into the river, and, of course, in our minds it still rides the roads, a ghost bus, appearing from nowhere, vanishing in a cloud of dust.

PS: There were many lighter moments during our travels…

*Zoe (a local girl) to Dave: "Is it one bus on top of another?"

* Sally picking up a packet of chemical toilet cleaner – "Milk anyone?"

* When I met an English barman at St Catherine's English club, I said: "You must know English beer then?"

He replied: "Yes, I lived there for a long time."

"What did you think of Newcastle," I said, meaning the famous Brown Ale."

"Never been North of Leeds," he replied.

*Jack Hayward, proudly showing us around his Montana Old People's Home – "We want to show you how we look after our aged. Of course, they have to have money in the first place."

*Chap to Roger, who was sticking a huge Union Jack to the front of the bus – "Are you from the States?"

*...like when we found the beer so expensive at the Hollywood Knickerbocker Hotel that we shared a half-pint between three.

*...like eating ice cream with a fork on the bus because we had run out of spoons.

*...like emptying our food leftovers on top of a bag full of grapefruit thinking it was a trash bag.

*...like when Roger leant so hard on his knife trying to cut a chunk off a steak at the Regents Park Hotel that the plate broke in half and his dinner ended up in his lap!

THE SIR GEORGE WHITE SPECIAL MEDIA COVERAGE

The big red bus with its intrepid young British crew attracted media attention wherever it travelled in North and South America and here are just a few of the headlines it attracted.

Correo

S/.2.00

Director: RONALD COLOMA HERRER
Empresa Periodística Nacional S.A.
Oficina de Redacción y Talleres
Ica 782 y 772 — Piura.
Av. Garcilaso de la Vega 1249 — Lima

OMNIBUS DE DOS PISOS PARALIZO TRANSITO

7dias

DEL PERÚ Y DEL MUNDO

Lima 1971 — octubre 22 — Nº 694 — año XX

Desde Inglaterra en Bus...

El Sol de México

Miembro de la Organización Periodística GARCÍA VALSECA

José García Valseca
PRESIDENTE Y DIRECTOR

MEXICO, D. F., Miércoles 17 de Junio de 1970 | No. 1673

AÑO V

Un Camión y Once Trotamundos

- Un Policía, su Novia y 9 Ingleses más
- Durante dos Años, Libres Como el Viento
- Brasil, Gran Favorito, Pero...
- El Mundial, en su Etapa Crítica

Viene de la Primera Página

Ella telefonista.

Planearon comprar un transporte entre todos y se hicieron de una unidad del servicio urbano del puerto de Bristol, de dos pisos, que les costó el equivalente a 8 mil pesos mexicanos. Gastaron otros 6 mil en las llantas y lo adaptaron. La parte baja para cocina y comedor, la alto, como dormitorio separado por cortinas. Total 500 libras esterlinas redondas.

pulsaron a mí a hacer el largo viaje —nos dice—, pero si he de ser sincero, desconozco las de mis compañeros. Pero supongo que cada uno tiene razones distintas.

Roger, el policía, quería olvidarse de estar en un crucero y... disfrutar de su luna de miel, porque iba a casarse con Bernice.

Don y Joan querían amplitud de horizontes, llenarse de espacios y de azul.

John, el periodista, calmar la inquietud reporteril de ir al fondo del co-

UNA PARTE DEL GRUPO de "Los Once" acompañados por la Sra. de Fernández, al centro y con el sombrerito negro. Están junto al chico mimado de la expedición: el transporte rojo de dos pisos. (Foto de Eduardo G. Gómez).

ONE WORLD EXPO
BRISTOL ENGLAND

Ten Young English People On Brookings Beach In Bri

By Evelyn Bieberdorf

A bright red, British double-decker bus has taken up temporary residence on the beach at Sporthaven Park near the south jetty of the Chetco

velopment of Englands highway system.

Roger Poole, leader of the group, and his wife are making the tour their honeymoon, as they were married a week prior to leaving England. Another

self-contained. The up deck is used for sle ing and the lower contains living quarte kitchenette and lavato Because of its height, feet, four inches, group must check cle

Recorrieron 45,000 kilómetros

En Amotape culminó raid de ingleses

LA NACIÓN

San José, Costa Rica - Miércoles 28 de julio de 1971 - Año XXIV - Nº 8.109 - Precio ¢ 0,40

ta al mundo en bus de

sos realizan 8 ingleses

Diario
de COSTA RICA

Directores: Julio Suñol — José María Penabad

Año LXXXV — Miércoles 28 de julio de 1971 — Nº 19.717

La vuelta al
mundo en bus
de dos pisos

The San Diego Union

EVENING OUTLOOK

95th Year—178th Issue   FOUNDED 1875   28 PAGES—10¢

1540 Third Street— EXbrook 4-6731, UPton 6-5527—Classified GL 1-1381 (C) 1970, United Western Newspapers, Inc.
Member of Associated Press, United Press International, Audit Bureau of Circulations

SANTA MONICA, CALIFORNIA, MONDAY, JULY 27, 1970

The  News

President
Rómulo O'Farrill, Sr.

Vol. XXI No. 355

Vice President and Editor-in-Chief
Rómulo O'Farrill, Jr.

Editado por el Diario Novedades. — Registrado como artículo de segunda clase
el 29 de octubre de 1955 en la administración de Correos de México, D. F.

Mexico City, Wednesday, June 30, 1971

Two-Story Bus Travels

Star &  Herald

ESTABLISHED IN 1849

"FOR THE CAUSE THAT LACKS ASSISTANCE; FOR THE FUTURE IN THE DISTANCE;
FOR THE WRONG THAT NEEDS RESISTANCE; AND THE GOOD THAT I CAN DO."

World Travelers Pick Apples In Oregon
Oranges In Florida To Swell Funds For Trip

BRISTOL HERALD COURIER

Combined Sundays With The

BRISTOL VIRGINIA-TENNESSEAN

BUS IS TOO TALL,
BUT WELCOME EMBRACES ALL

By LESLIE BERKMAN
Register-Examiner Staff Writer

...ing British adventurers are

attracted curious onlookers and wellwishers.
"Some people seem to wonder if it is real and
if it is how did it get here?" Conway observes.

championships, they enjoyed the same welcome.

But traveling in an oversized bus can lead

wide, 14-foot six-in...
higher than the m...
mitted on freeways...

276